RIGHTEOUSNESS IN THE MARKETPLACE

RECLAIMING YOUR WORK FROM HUSTLE AND PERFORMANCE

FE D. JONES

Righteousness in the Marketplace: Reclaiming Your Work from Hustle and Performance

Copyright © 2026 by Fe D. Jones

All rights reserved.

Published by Radical Lives Press

RadicalLives.com

First edition, 2026

No part of this publication may be reproduced, stored in a retrieval system, or transmitted in any form or by any means, electronic, mechanical, photocopying, recording, or otherwise, without the prior written permission of the publisher, except for brief quotations used in reviews, articles, or teaching materials with proper citation.

Unless otherwise indicated, Scripture quotations are taken from the Holy Bible, New Living Translation (NLT), copyright © 1996, 2004, 2015 by Tyndale House Foundation. Used by permission of Tyndale House Publishers, Carol Stream, Illinois 60188. All rights reserved.

ISBN (print): ISBN: 979-8-9987542-0-3

ISBN (eBook): ISBN: 979-8-9987542-1-0

Cover and interior design by Fe D. Jones

For permissions, bulk orders, or inquiries, contact:

info@fejoneslive.com

Disclaimer

This book is intended for educational and spiritual development purposes only. The author and publisher have prepared this content to provide biblical insight, mindset coaching, and practical encouragement based on personal experience, professional training, and scriptural interpretation. It is not intended to replace legal, financial, therapeutic, or professional business advice.

The principles outlined in this book are presented from a faith-based perspective and reflect the convictions and lived experiences of the author. Readers are encouraged to pray, seek wise counsel, and apply discernment when making personal or professional decisions.

Any business strategies, examples, or testimonials referenced in this work are illustrative in nature and do not guarantee specific results. The outcomes you experience will depend on your unique effort, obedience, and alignment with God's timing and purpose for your life and business.

All coaching methodologies, mindset frameworks, journal prompts, teaching sequences, and strategy models included in this book are the intellectual property of the author and Radical Lives. These materials may not be copied, reproduced, taught, or integrated into other programs, courses, or commercial offerings without prior written consent.

The author and Radical Lives assume no liability for how the information in this book is applied or interpreted.

This book may contain references to third-party organizations, services, or products. These are included for informational purposes only and do not constitute endorsements.

TABLE OF CONTENTS

THE COMMISSION _____ 1

Part I - Foundation of the Call

Burn the Blueprint _____ 10

Righteous, Not Religious _____ 52

The Lie of the Industry Standard _____ 108

Part II - Refining the Builder

What Integrity Costs (and What It's Worth) _____ 130

Righteousness Isn't a Marketing Strategy _____ 147

Righteousness Protects the Sacred _____ 179

Part III - Constructing with Heaven's Pattern

Wholeness Makes You Wise _____ 215

Righteousness in the Supply Chain _____ 244

Wisdom in the Digital Age _____ 272

Part IV - The Final Audit

The Unseen Fruit of Righteous Work _____ 316

What Will Heaven Say About What You Built? ___ 342

THE COMMISSION

I took a deep breath and pushed the button. The screen said, "Submitted." I exhaled all of the tension that had been built up for the last seven weeks. My back melts into the chair as I exhale the words "It is finished."

I sat there for a good fifteen minutes contemplating what I had just submitted. It weighed heavy on my heart. It wasn't just a paper but rather a message waiting to be shared. Eager to wash the weight of the words that still trembled in every fiber of my body, I resort to the waterfall shower head. Warm water cleansing my soul from head to toe when suddenly I hear a voice whisper, "Righteousness in the marketplace."

The voice is a voice I'm well acquainted with. It is the voice that was there with me when I thought I was taking my last breath as a result of an overdose at age 16, and the voice that guided me through the motorcycle accident I had in 2020.

It's a voice that loves truth. Stern but loving. Challenging but kind. Persistent yet so quiet it can only be heard when we still the chaos of the mind.

It is the voice of a person who is always there, ready to instill wisdom and insight at a moment's notice. I call that voice the Breath of Life.

At that moment I knew what had just transpired. It wasn't just a random thought but rather a commission from the Divine. A green light to champion this message to breathe life upon the weary souls who feel as if they're dying a slow painful death at the hands of the dopamine addiction of follows and likes.

The souls who are fighting for their dream to build a business yet feel as if they have to prostitute their gift to get paid. Life for the one who deep down inside knows there is a better way to do business. A way that may seem old-fashioned today but it's been tried and true through the ages.

As the months progressed, as a woman with child, what was once a tiny seed now has movement. There's an internal wrestling within my womb of a message in formation, growing, developing each day but not yet ready to be birthed.

Fighting for space, I can feel its every turn. The jab on my side, the deep stretch that leads to a sudden groan. There's a part of me that wants to hurry up and get this over with so I can feel relief, but as a mother incubating their child, I know that releasing the message prematurely can lead to an underdeveloped message that can die before it even gets the chance.

The only difference is this message is not a nine-month deal. No, I was birthing an elephant. Twenty-two months of continuous movement before I was happy with the first words inked on this paper. Only to realize it wasn't true labor after all. This baby needed a little more time.

So here I am on the birthing floor, finally pushing out the child we have all been waiting for, nearly two years into the journey.

That message of hope, warning, and confirmation for many that what your soul has been craving and gravitating to has not been the late-night pizza talking but rather the Breath of Life itself whispering the message of truth into your ear.

And now that the message has found its moment, you're being invited into something deeper. This isn't just my birthing story. It's your permission slip. Your confirmation. Your call to come out from under the weight of the world's strategies and into the shelter of God's blueprint. Every chapter ahead will stretch you and strip you. It will challenge the ways you've learned to survive and

provoke the parts of you that are still hustling in fear. But if you let it, this message will also cleanse you. It will clarify what matters, restore what's sacred, and show you how to build something that heaven can endorse.
So take this slow. Don't race through it. Read it like it was written, for your realignment, for your freedom, and for your legacy.

Let's build what God can bless.

PART I - FOUNDATION OF THE CALL

CHAPTER 1

BURN THE BLUEPRINT

THE STRATEGY ISN'T SACRED

You can't build a holy business without the Holy Spirit.

Not a program.

Not a prophetic word.

Not a mastermind group.

The only blueprint that matters is the one heaven gave you, and if you're not in constant intimacy with the Spirit of God, then you're not building in alignment. You're building in assumption.

And let's be clear, this conversation is not about throwing out every system and method the world has developed. We live in the world. We use tools from the world. But we are not of it. And if we forget that, we'll start calling things "strategy" that God calls sin. We'll baptize ambition and call it faith. We'll embrace shortcuts that look smart but carry spiritual death.

Take AI for example. Some Christians are ready to toss it all out and label it as the mark of the beast. But that's short-sighted. Yes, the antichrist will use every system, technology, food, housing, even medicine, to control and manipulate. But that doesn't mean we can't use those same tools in this window of time to do the opposite: to build with purity, to communicate with clarity, to advance the kingdom instead of ourselves.

But that only works when everything we build is filtered through scripture and tested in the presence of God. Tools don't make something righteous. Alignment does.

I've spent the last fifteen years in the business world. I've done the coaching. I've taken the courses. I've studied under well-known names and lesser-known experts. And while I've learned a lot, I've also seen too much. I've seen new age practices covered in Christian language. I've seen greed and gluttony preached from platforms while using God's name as a sales hook. And I've seen people, some sincere, some not, prostituting their gift for influence, income, or identity.

The truth is, gluttony is not just about food. It's the overconsumption of anything that keeps you from being sensitive to the Holy Spirit. It crowds Him out. It dulls your discernment. And when that happens, you stop asking the right questions. You stop listening. You stop seeking. And before you know it, you're no longer in a holy partnership. You're in a personal project that uses God's name but ignores His voice.

I'm not writing this to tear down those who are trying to figure it out. I'm writing this to call us back to the One who never needed a launch strategy to change the world. I'm writing this as a prophet who hears the assignment loud and clear: to protect your intimacy with God, even if it means saying what no one else will.

This chapter is not about fear. It's about reverence. It's about slowing down long enough to ask, am I building something God can bless, or am I just building something that works?

WHEN HUNGER BECOMES HERESY

Idolatry isn't always a golden calf. Sometimes it's a golden strategy.

Sometimes it looks like hustle. Sometimes it sounds like mentorship. Sometimes it hides behind a spreadsheet, a coaching program, a prophetic word wrapped in self-promotion.

But from Genesis to Revelation, God is clear about how He sees it.

He doesn't call it misalignment. He calls it adultery.

> *"YOU ARE AN ADULTEROUS WIFE WHO TAKES IN STRANGERS INSTEAD OF HER OWN HUSBAND."*
> *, EZEKIEL 16:32 (NLT)*

To God, idolatry is betrayal. And when we elevate anything, any person, platform, or plan, above His voice, we are not just out of order. We are out of covenant. We're cheating on the One who gave us breath and calling it business.

In today's marketplace, even among Christians, idolatry wears makeup.

We give spiritual-sounding language to secular systems. We elevate business gurus as if their words are infallible and untouchable, ignoring the Berean model of Acts 17:11, where the people searched the Scriptures to test even what Paul taught. We use phrases like "kingdom strategy" to endorse ambition and justify mixture. We disguise profit motives as prophetic mandates and turn the marketplace into a stage where God's name is mentioned, but His character is missing.

I've watched leaders instruct people not to create their own books, courses, or content unless they were directly copying the "approved" model. I've seen believers claim their material was divinely downloaded, while simultaneously pressuring others to purchase or risk "missing out on what God is doing." This isn't biblical mentorship. It's spiritual manipulation. And it leads to something even more dangerous: performance-based faith.

The Holy Spirit convicted me deeply in this area, not in a single moment, but over time. When I finally sat down with my Bible, my journal, and my raw honesty, I realized something. I had never been chasing fame. I wasn't addicted to applause. I was longing for legacy. I wanted to build something that would outlive me. Something my great-great-grandchildren could still learn from, still be shaped by. But legacy without obedience is just ego in disguise. And God showed me clearly that only what is rooted in Him will remain.

> "SEEK THE KINGDOM OF GOD ABOVE ALL ELSE, AND LIVE RIGHTEOUSLY, AND HE WILL GIVE YOU EVERYTHING YOU NEED."
> , MATTHEW 6:33 (NLT)

This scripture became my foundation. But God didn't let me quote it casually. He took me into the original languages.

Before we move further, I want to clarify something that will show up throughout this book. You'll notice I reference both Greek and Hebrew Strong's definitions, but in many cases, I return to the Hebrew root, even for New Testament scriptures. That's intentional. The writers of the New Testament were Hebrew men. Their worldview, their vocabulary, and their understanding of spiritual concepts were rooted in Torah. So even when they spoke or wrote in Greek, the meanings they carried were informed by Hebrew culture, covenant, and mindset. To fully understand a word like kingdom or righteousness, we can't just rely on Greek translation, we have to return to Hebrew foundation. That's how we recover not just the word, but the motive behind the word. The spirit of what was being said. That's how we rightly divide truth.

Strong's Breakdown:

- "Kingdom" in Greek is basileia (G932), meaning realm, reign, or royal rule. It's not just a place. It's a posture.
- The contrasting Greek word kosmos (G2889), used elsewhere in the New Testament, refers to the systems, values, and order of the world.
- To "seek first" the Kingdom is to seek God's intentional rule over every area of your life, not just in theory, but in strategy, stewardship, and sacrifice.

And what does it mean to "live righteously"?

The word "righteousness" in Greek is dikaiosunē (G1343), but let's go deeper. In Hebrew, the word for righteousness is "tsedeq" (צֶדֶק) , Strong's H6664.

The pictograph meaning breaks down as:

צ (Tsade) = a fishhook or desire

ד (Dalet) = a door or pathway

ק (Qof) = the back of the head, or what's behind

Put together, it shows a person being drawn through a door by what is unseen, walking by faith, not by sight, and being led into alignment with God's mind and heart. Righteousness is not just about moral behavior. It's about correct positioning. It's about choosing God's way even when the world's way is faster, flashier, or more profitable.

This is what I had to face.

I had been diligent. I had studied. I had invested time and money into coaching, branding, marketing, but I had to admit, I had also adopted systems that weren't just flawed, they were flesh-driven. I was participating in hustle culture, calling it excellence. I was following formulas that elevated visibility over vision. And somewhere in the noise, I had stopped checking in with God.

But the Spirit didn't shame me. He revealed truth, and truth set me free. One of the biggest breakthroughs came through understanding a lesser-known passage in Proverbs:

> *"WHEN YOU SIT TO DINE WITH A RULER, NOTE WELL WHAT IS BEFORE YOU, AND PUT A KNIFE TO YOUR THROAT IF YOU ARE GIVEN TO GLUTTONY. DO NOT CRAVE HIS DELICACIES, FOR THAT FOOD IS DECEPTIVE."*
> *, PROVERBS 23:1–3 (NLT)*

The word "gluttony" here ties to the Hebrew Strong's H2151, which carries a meaning of insatiable appetite, indulgence, or overconsumption.

But even deeper, the Hebrew word for "appetite" in verse 2 is nephesh (Strong's H5315), the same word used for soul. This shows us that gluttony is not just a physical sin. It's a soul-level distortion.

When our appetites are unchecked, they pull us away from discernment. And in business, that appetite might not be for food. It could be for influence, money, validation, revenge, or recognition. Whatever controls your appetite, controls your altar.

That brings us back to one of the most misquoted, underestimated verses in the Bible:

> *"FOR THE LOVE OF MONEY IS THE ROOT OF ALL KINDS OF EVIL."*
> *, 1 TIMOTHY 6:10 (NLT)*

Let's break this down the way the Spirit showed me:

- Love = ahavah (Hebrew Strong's H157): not just affection, but emotional attachment, longing, or even covenant-level connection
- Money = keseph (Hebrew Strong's H3701): silver, currency, but also symbolic of desire, lust, or craving in first-use Hebrew contexts

When we form a covenant with money, when it becomes the object of our trust, the driver of our decisions, the thing we're emotionally attached to, we are no longer servants of God. We are slaves to Mammon.

Jesus warned us plainly in Matthew 6:24: "You cannot serve both God and money."

And the Holy Spirit made it clear to me, if your business decisions are being driven by your fears, your bills, or your ego, then God is not the CEO of your company. You are.

That's when everything shifted.

I stopped chasing strategies and started pressing into intimacy. I restructured my business model to reflect God's character, not just His blessings. I no longer cared about being algorithm-friendly. I cared about being heaven-approved. I no longer needed to go viral. I wanted to be valid in the Spirit.

Because at the end of it all, what does it profit a woman to gain the world's attention and lose her soul?

God reminded me, He is the only boss you can work for and not realize you've been fired.

And I refused to keep building if heaven had already exited the project.

THE IMPOSTOR GOSPEL

You can't build what God can bless if you're still performing for approval. That may sound harsh, but it's true. And here's the problem: most Christian women don't even realize they're performing. They've mistaken the grind for obedience. They've confused exhaustion with faithfulness. They've accepted manipulation as marketing and called it strategy. But underneath all of that? There's a silent epidemic happening in the soul. A craving to be seen, heard, validated, and it all comes from one core issue:

THEY DON'T KNOW WHO THEY ARE.

When you don't know your identity, you become vulnerable to counterfeit gospels. You adopt strategies that contradict your values. You mirror behavior that doesn't match your convictions. You build brands that look right, but don't feel right. You say it's for the Kingdom, but deep down, you're hoping it gets you clout, likes, or applause. Not because you're evil. Not because you're manipulative. But because you've never been taught how to build from alignment. And I get it. I've lived it.

For years, I didn't know who I was. I grew up in church, literally since I was two months old. But I didn't encounter God for myself until I was lying in a hospital bed after a drug overdose. That moment changed everything. It awakened something real in me. But even after that radical encounter, I didn't know what it meant to walk in identity. I only knew how to walk in performance.

When I moved to Puerto Rico as a teenager and joined a holiness Pentecostal church, I encountered a religious spirit masked as righteousness. Don't get me wrong, Pentecost is real. Holiness is essential. The Holy Spirit is alive and active. But in the specific circle I was in, holiness was defined by rules, not relationship. Long skirts, no makeup, no nail polish, no pants. Appearance over intimacy. External compliance over internal transformation. As a cosmetologist and nail tech in training, I was immediately labeled a problem. The bright colors on my nails, the heels I wore, the makeup I applied, it wasn't just personal expression. To them, it was rebellion. I was called a Jezebel. And because I was young, impressionable, and desperate to do things "right," I complied. I changed how I dressed. I silenced parts of myself. I followed every rule. But here's the truth:

THERE WAS NO REAL TRANSFORMATION IN MY HEART.

I looked the part. I talked the part. But I was living from fear, not faith. I had learned how to perform. Not how to be. And that's exactly what many women do when they enter the marketplace. They translate that same religious performance into business performance. They post for the algorithm instead of for God. They build brands that reflect what's trending, not what's true. They create content for likes, not legacy. And slowly, silently, they drift into living for the 'Gram instead of living for Christ.

They say things like:

- "I need to keep up."
- "This would make great content."
- "I have to show them I'm successful."
- "Let me make this aesthetic."
- "If I don't do it like her, I won't grow."

But what they don't realize is that they're not marketing, they're begging to be seen. This is what I call performance addiction. And it's not just a habit. It's a stronghold. One that's deeply tied to the brain's reward system, where dopamine spikes every time someone likes, comments, follows, or buys. That hit of validation feels like purpose. But it's not. It's a pacifier. A shallow substitute for the deep knowing that only comes from identity in Christ. And here's the part no one tells you:

Sometimes, the performance doesn't look flashy. Sometimes, it's not about filters and aesthetics. Sometimes, the performance shows up as over-delivering, under-pricing, saying yes to everything, doubting your authority, refusing to rest, obsessing over reviews, and secretly hoping your clients will "like" you more than they respect you.

And it's all rooted in the same lie:

"Who I am is not enough."

But let me give you some truth. The Hebrew word God used to describe woman in Genesis wasn't some passive assistant role. It was "ezer kenegdo." And it's one of the most powerful terms in scripture.

Ezer = helper, ally, rescuer.

Kenegdo = corresponding to, equal and opposite to, standing face to face.

This phrase doesn't mean you were created to serve silently in the background. It means you were designed to stand face to face with problems and bring divine solutions. It's the same word used to describe how God comes to Israel's rescue in times of war.

So what does that mean for your business? It means you don't have to compromise.

You don't need manipulation.

You don't have to hustle until your soul is numb.

You don't have to water down your voice, copy someone else's strategy, or dress your trauma up in branding just to feel valid.

You're already the solution.

The key is learning how to live from that truth.

But how?

You start by discovering your identity. And that discovery requires more than just quoting scriptures, it demands introspection. This is where journaling becomes spiritual warfare. As you pour out your thoughts, desires, wounds, and dreams onto the page, the Holy Spirit begins to highlight who He created you to be. He shows you your wiring. Your rhythm. Your divine design.

For example: you've probably noticed by now that this chapter doesn't ease you in softly. I'm not here for fluff. This isn't feel-good encouragement or Instagram captions repackaged as a book. This is transformation on paper. That's how I'm wired. I write like I coach, bold, layered, no-nonsense. And I do it that way because I know who I am.

When you know who you are, you stop building for optics and start building from overflow.

You stop living life by default and start living life by design.

That's what internal alignment looks like. You're not tossed by trends. You're not chasing gurus. You're not mimicking methods that worked for someone else.

You're rooted. You're still. You're clear.

And you're dangerous to the enemy because you're no longer trying to be seen, you're already known.

And yes, obedience still requires action. But that action flows from love, not fear. From confidence, not chaos. From vision, not performance.

Alignment will not always lead to instant success. It may not make you rich in 30 days. But it will make you righteous. And when God sees that He can trust you, He starts to release more. More resources. More wisdom. More responsibility. Not because you earned it, but because you were ready to steward it.

And that starts right here.

In the quiet.

In the journaling.

In the healing.

In the dismantling of every counterfeit gospel you've unknowingly lived.

Because the only thing worse than building a successful business...

is building one that cost you your soul.

THE IDOL IN THE MIRROR

Before I realized I was performing, I just thought I was working hard.

I wasn't building out of rebellion. I was building out of fear. A deep, unspoken fear that if I didn't succeed, if I didn't "make it", then the people who hurt me would be right. That everything they said about me was true. That I really wouldn't amount to anything. So I hustled to prove myself, not to strangers, but to the people whose words had pierced the deepest: family. Critics. Old voices still echoing in the corners of my soul. The people who rejected me. The ones who misunderstood me. The ones who made me feel like I didn't belong.

I was striving to be seen by people who didn't even know how to see themselves. And that's what makes it dangerous, because when you don't know your identity, you look for mirrors in broken places. You perform for the applause of people who haven't healed themselves. You hunger for validation from people who are still running from their own purpose. And somewhere along the way, you convince yourself that success will heal the wound. But it doesn't.

Success doesn't heal rejection. It only hides it.

And if you don't let God deal with the root, you'll build your whole business around the ache of being unseen.

I had to confront something most people don't want to admit: I was living in fantasy. Not the kind you see in movies, but the kind that forms in the heart of a child who grows up feeling neglected, misunderstood, or emotionally invisible. It's the fantasy that one day, you'll finally be validated. That one day, your parents will see you, support you, cheer you on. That one day, you'll be celebrated by the people who once wounded you.

It's a fantasy built on hope. But sometimes, hope becomes a prison when it's tied to people who can't give you what you need. And I had to grieve that. I had to sit with the possibility that the apology might never come. That the celebration might never happen. That the family dynamic I longed for might never be restored the way I imagined.

And when I finally let go of that fantasy, something beautiful happened:

I STARTED TO SEE ME.

I started to see the gifts, the wiring, the voice, and the power God had placed inside of me. And not just see them, but honor them. I saw how every hardship had left a tool in my toolbox. Every valley had deposited something I needed for my calling. Every painful experience had equipped me for the very thing I was now being called to build.

And the first strategy I implemented after that breakthrough?

BOUNDARIES.

Before, I built walls. Walls to keep people out. But walls also keep you locked in. They isolate. They harden. They suffocate. Boundaries, on the other hand, are wise. They are sacred lines of love. They tell the truth about what is acceptable and what is not, without shutting down intimacy or community.

And before I could set boundaries with other people, I had to set them with myself.

I had to stop apologizing for taking up space.

I had to stop explaining why I thought differently.

I had to stop shrinking to make others feel safe.

I had to stop bending my convictions for the sake of optics.

I had to stop outsourcing my decisions to culture, family, and tradition.

In short, I had to stop betraying myself. Because that's what happens when we don't know who we are. We betray ourselves to gain approval. We silence our voice to be accepted. We water down our message to be liked. And we call it "strategy," when it's actually spiritual sabotage.

But when I started honoring my own voice, when I committed to follow what God put in me, no matter who misunderstood, I found peace.

NOT COMFORT. NOT EASE. NOT APPLAUSE.
PEACE.

And with peace came clarity. With clarity came strategy. And with strategy came authority.

I no longer had to build out of desperation. I could build from a place of rest. And that rest made room for God to move, not just in my business, but in me.

People who respected me started learning how to honor the boundaries I set. Some took time, but they adapted. And the ones who didn't? I didn't have to push them out of my life. They faded on their own.

Because healthy boundaries have a way of exposing unhealthy patterns, and when the manipulation doesn't work anymore, the manipulators lose interest.

I also had to stop taking responsibility for other people's reactions. That was a big one. Let me be clear: I'm not talking about being rude, cold, or callous. I'm talking about communicating clearly, with honor and love, and then letting people own their own responses.

If someone throws a guilt trip, gets defensive, or lashes out in manipulation when you express your boundaries with grace, that's not your monkey, and it's not your circus. Enforce the boundary. Stay firm. Let them sit in the discomfort. Because that discomfort might just be the very thing God uses to convict and correct them.

You cannot be both obedient and addicted to approval.

You cannot protect your purpose and your image at the same time.

And you cannot make disciples while still trying to win over the people who crucified your confidence.

Once I let go of that idol, of trying to be everything for everyone, I started to trust my own judgment. I stopped second-guessing what I knew God told me. I stopped asking permission from people who were never called to steward my assignment. And I started walking like someone who had been sent, not just saved.

And that's when I understood something deep:

Righteousness in the Marketplace

My voice carries a sound.

And it's not for everyone.

There is a tribe God has called me to. A group of women who hear what I say and feel something shake loose in their soul. And for them, my sound is healing. It's clarity. It's confirmation.

But for others, it may irritate. It may confront. It may even repel.

And that's okay.

Because I'm not a $100 bill.

Like my great-grandmother used to say, even a hundred-dollar bill doesn't fit perfectly in every pocket. Not everyone is going to carry you. Not everyone is supposed to. Not everyone will receive you. But the ones who are called to you? They'll recognize your voice in a crowd. They'll find your sound in the noise. And they'll thank God for the freedom it brings.

So I bless the ones who can't receive me.

I release the ones who don't get it.

And I walk in peace, because the only eyes I'm trying to catch are His.

Dig Deeper:

You've made it this far, which means you're not just skimming for inspiration. You're ready for transformation.
This isn't about adjusting your strategy. It's about confronting your spiritual architecture. So before you keep building, answer these in the quiet place with God. Grab a journal, or a notebook, and begin to respond as if you're speaking directly to the One who knows you best. Let the Holy Spirit search the blueprint.

1. Who are you trying to prove yourself to, and why do they still have that much

power in your life?

What fantasy are you still holding onto?

2. Have you built your business (or your brand) around being seen… or being obedient?

Would you still do it if no one clapped?

3. Are your boundaries a reflection of your healing, or your trauma?

Are you avoiding confrontation… or honoring your design?

4. What does your content, lifestyle, and presence online truly preach?

Would someone see Christ in you, or just the curated version of who you think you need to be?

5. Where do you need to release control and ask God to burn the old blueprint?

What strategy, standard, or identity needs to be surrendered so you can build what God can actually bless?

Prayer Activation

Father,

I lift up this daughter of Yours who has been performing for far too long. She's been building on the approval of man, the pressure of culture, and the echoes of past rejection. But today, in the name of Jesus, I ask that You begin to release her from every lie, every idol, every false identity, and every fantasy that has kept her bound.

Open her eyes to see where the enemy has stolen her clarity.

Expose the blueprints she's adopted that You never authored.

Reveal to her where hustle has replaced holiness.

Where branding has replaced boldness.

Where people-pleasing has replaced Your presence.

Holy Spirit, overtake her right now. Let Your truth pierce through the fog. Let Your presence flood the room where she is sitting. Wrap her in the security of knowing that You see her, You chose her, and You love her too much to let her keep building on sand.

God, I ask that You speak her name the way You whispered it before the foundations of the earth. Remind her of who she is. Show her the gift You placed in her hands. Resurrect the pieces of her identity that trauma buried. And restore her boldness to walk in what You called her to do, without apology, without pretense, without fear.

Give her the courage to grieve what she never had.

The strength to release what no longer fits.

The fire to set boundaries without guilt.

And the faith to burn the old blueprint, so she can finally build what You can bless.

In Jesus' name,

Amen.

THE BLUEPRINT IS BURNING

You don't need another formula.

You don't need another mentor.

You don't need another motivational quote.

You need to burn the blueprint.

The one built on performance.

The one soaked in people-pleasing.

The one shaped by rejection, fantasy, and fear.

God is not blessing what you're building if you're building it from bondage.

And you already know that. That's why you're still reading.

This chapter wasn't just words. It was a breaking. A divine disruption.

And now the fire's been lit. You can't unsee what's been revealed.

You can't unknow what the Holy Spirit just confirmed.

So what will you do with it?

You're not just a business owner. You're a builder of altars.

Every offer you create, every brand you shape, every message you release, either draws people closer to the Father or lures them toward idolatry. There is no middle ground.

But here's the good news: you were made for righteousness.

The real you, the one God designed before time, was built with fire in her bones and truth in her mouth.

She doesn't compromise. She doesn't water it down. She doesn't trade her birthright for branding.

And she's rising now.

Not to prove herself. Not to please the crowd. But to walk in alignment.

To build what God can bless.

To leave behind the sand and stand on the Rock.

To say with every fiber of her being: "God, I'm done with the world's plans. I want Your design."

So burn the blueprint.

Let the fire fall.

And watch what He builds through your ashes.

CHAPTER 2

RIGHTEOUS, NOT RELIGIOUS

"God never called us to perform holiness, He called us to embody it. Righteousness builds altars. Religion builds platforms."

THE SPIRIT BEHIND THE STRATEGY

It's easy to confuse righteousness with religion until you see them side by side. At a glance, both can look "holy." Both can quote scripture. Both can stand behind a pulpit or write books. But if you lean in long enough, you'll sense it: one is rooted in intimacy, the other in image.

Religion performs. Righteousness aligns.

Religion wants to be seen. Righteousness wants to be surrendered.

The core difference is relationship.

A woman walking in righteousness isn't perfect, but she's deeply connected to the One who is. She walks with conviction, but not with pride. Her boldness doesn't come from spiritual superiority, it flows from knowing God's heart. Righteousness is anchored in humility. It's a quiet but firm reverence for God's standard, and a deep understanding that being used by Him is not a badge of honor, it's a sacred assignment.

On the other hand, religion is performance-driven. It feeds on control, image, and appearances. It masks insecurity with spiritual pride and seeks applause instead of transformation. When the spotlight shifts or their perfection is questioned, religious spirits become hostile. Why? Because their identity is rooted in how they're seen, not in who they serve.

You can always identify religion by the fruit. Religion resists correction. It clings to its platform. It weaponizes scripture to protect ego instead of humbling the heart. The Pharisees were the perfect example of this spirit in action.

- They elevated tradition over truth.
- They prioritized rules over relationship.
- They burdened people with legalism but refused to lift a finger to help.
- They performed righteousness outwardly, but their hearts were far from God.

(Matthew 23 offers a full breakdown, and if you read it with spiritual eyes, it exposes the same patterns we still see today.)

But righteousness? Righteousness is relational. It seeks to walk in right standing with God and others. Not for image. Not for networking. But because the heart of righteousness is reconciliation. It's being a peacekeeper without compromising truth. It's understanding that how we treat people is a direct reflection of how we reverence God.

The woman walking in righteousness doesn't need to be loud. She doesn't need the stage. She doesn't need the last word. Her power isn't in performance. It's in purity.

And purity doesn't mean perfection, it means surrender.

When righteousness shows up in business, it doesn't just shape what we build. It purifies how we build it. Our marketing becomes less manipulative and more meaningful. Our offers carry integrity. Our voice carries weight, not because it's clever, but because it's clean. When we walk in righteousness, we do the right thing even when no one is watching. Especially when no one is watching.

Because we're not moved by optics. We're moved by obedience.

The woman who is righteous will not sacrifice her assignment on the altar of ambition.

And that's what separates her from the one who's religious.

Because religion is about self-worship.

Righteousness is about surrender.

And one of them builds a platform.

The other builds an altar.

GOD'S STANDARD STILL STANDS

Righteousness isn't behavior management.

It's not religious appearance.

It's not Christian branding.

Righteousness is relational alignment.

It's living in sync with God's heart, God's

mind, and God's design, even when nobody's watching.

And while religion teaches us how to look holy, righteousness teaches us how to be holy.

At the core of this is a verse you've already seen in Chapter 1, but it's one we can't afford to skim past:

> **MATTHEW 6:33.** "SEEK THE KINGDOM OF GOD ABOVE ALL ELSE, AND LIVE RIGHTEOUSLY, AND HE WILL GIVE YOU EVERYTHING YOU NEED." (NLT)

This isn't a motivational verse, it's a blueprint. A divine sequence.

Seek first what? The Kingdom of God and His righteousness.

Then what? "All these things", your needs, your provisions, your resources, "will be added unto you."

Let's break it open again.

The Greek word for "Kingdom" here is basileia (Strong's G932), which refers to God's royal rule, authority, and dominion. But to truly understand what Jesus meant, we must remember who He was speaking to, Hebrew people, steeped in Torah. His words weren't random. They were rooted.

So we go back further, to the Hebrew mindset and original language, and we see the deeper layers.

When Jesus said righteousness, He wasn't referring to self-righteousness or rule-following. The Greek word used is dikaiosynē (Strong's G1343), which means equity of character or act; right standing with God; the condition acceptable to Him. But even deeper than that, when we follow the law of first mention and examine the Hebrew foundation, we get a more complete picture.

In Hebrew, the word for righteousness is tsedeq (Strong's H6664), rooted in justice, fairness, and right relationship. And in the Hebrew pictographs:

- Tzadé (צ) – A fishhook, representing desire or need.
- Dalet (ד) – A door, symbolizing access, movement, or decision.
- Qof (ק) – The back of the head, representing what's behind or what follows.

Put together, tsedeq gives us a stunning picture:

"The desire that leads us through the door and changes what follows."

Righteousness is not static. It moves you. It changes you.

It redirects your desires and ushers you into a lifestyle that reflects God's character.

So when Jesus said, "Seek first the Kingdom of God and His righteousness," what He was really saying is:

"Pursue God's dominion and His way of being. Pursue what's in His heart. Let that be the door that leads your decisions, and everything else will follow."

That's righteousness.

It means when we build a business, we're not just thinking about money, we're asking, "Does this reflect God's heart for people?"

It means we don't compromise our values to keep up with trends or appease audiences.

It means we check the spirit behind our strategy.

God will absolutely allow us to experience wealth and enjoy the fruit of our labor, but He's always going to ask:

"How does this advance My Kingdom?"

Not "How does it make you look?"

Not "How fast does it scale?"

But "How does it serve My people and reflect My ways?"

And here's the truth, serving God's people doesn't always look like preaching or evangelizing.

It might look like product quality.

It might look like timely delivery.

It might look like how you respond to a complaint, how you speak in your DMs, how you treat your team, or how you treat your competitor.

Are you leaving a bad taste in someone's mouth because you're bold in your faith, or because your customer service is poor?

Because here's the thing: righteousness shows up in your behavior, but it cannot be manufactured.

A narcissist can put on a performance. So can a religious spirit. But eventually, when the fuse blows or the pressure hits, the real self comes out. The cracks begin to show. The sharp tongue. The controlling attitude. The unkindness. The sarcasm. The self-pity. The passive-aggression. The refusal to take accountability.

Righteousness cannot be faked.

It isn't "niceness", which is often manipulative and rooted in self-gain.

It's kindness, which flows from alignment with God's character and is consistent no matter who's watching.

True righteousness becomes your default.

You show up in excellence not because of optics, but because it's your conviction.

You serve people well not for applause, but because it honors God.

And when people encounter that, it builds trust. And trust builds impact.

Think about the Samaritan. He didn't just help the wounded man, he left a deposit and promised to return with more. And the innkeeper agreed. Why? Because the Samaritan had a reputation. He had history. He was good on his word.

That's righteousness.

Joseph had the same track record. Betrayed, falsely accused, imprisoned, but righteous. When Pharaoh elevated him, it wasn't because Joseph networked or hustled. It was because he was trustworthy. His decisions honored God. And that consistency paved the way for divine promotion.

So the question is this:

Are we living that way?

Or are we dressing up our dysfunction in Christian language and calling it business? Because if we're building with God, then His standard still stands.

WHEN RELIGION BECOMES A MASK

Religion will teach you how to act the part. Righteousness will teach you how to be the part. And the truth is, most people can't tell the difference until it's too late, until the fruit has rotted, the foundation has cracked, and everything that looked good from the outside begins to smell like death on the inside.

It's not hard to spot the difference once your eyes have been opened. You begin to discern very quickly whether someone is serving God out of love or operating out of performance. And contrary to what some people think, this isn't about how they dress, whether or not they wear makeup, or how much scripture they can quote. The real markers of religion are pride, defensiveness, hostility toward correction, and a desperate need to be seen.

The Pharisees were masters of this kind of behavior. They loved the front row. They loved being greeted publicly and treated with reverence. But Jesus wasn't impressed. He called them out time and time again, not because they failed to follow God's law, but because they had no relationship with Him. Their hearts were far from the One they claimed to represent.

Let's look at some of the defining behaviors of the Pharisees:

- They were obsessed with appearances (Matthew 23:27-28). They wanted to look righteous, but were full of hypocrisy.
- They added burdens to people's spiritual lives while refusing to help them carry them (Matthew 23:4).

- They used the Word to manipulate, not to serve (Mark 7:8-13).
- They rejected correction and became enraged when their spiritual facades were challenged (Luke 11:45-54).
- They weaponized spiritual authority to protect their power, not to protect people (John 9:16, 34).

These traits didn't die with the Pharisees. They live on today, especially in business circles that have learned to cover manipulation and exploitation with scripture and spiritual language.

I remember being part of a very well-known insurance marketing organization, a huge name in the industry. On the surface, everything looked great. The culture was polished, professional, and driven by success. But once I got inside, I realized it was a different story.

Behind the motivational speeches and curated social media presence was a culture of pressure, manipulation, and division. People were being pitted against one another in a race to the top. There were subtle (and sometimes not-so-subtle) demands to compromise, ethically, emotionally, spiritually. There was gaslighting. Deception. Even illegal suggestions, dressed up as strategy.

And here's the worst part: for a minute, I tried to make it work. Not because I believed in what they were doing, but because I could see the reward on the other side. The money. The status. The visibility. The photos with high-level influencers. The doors it could open. I knew I could climb the ranks. I knew I had the capacity to make it to the top.

But at what cost?

See, this is where the love of money chokes out everything else. You don't feel it at first. It feels like motivation. Like drive. Like passion. But slowly, that breath of God inside you gets smothered. And before you know it, you're no longer building with God, you're building with greed. You're building with fear. You're building on fantasy.

The word "love" in 1 Timothy 6:10, "the love of money is the root of all kinds of evil", is so much deeper than emotion. In Hebrew, love (ahab, Strong's H157) means to breathe after. To long for. To cling to with intensity. Love gives life. But when directed at the wrong thing, it begins to destroy. To love money isn't just to want it. It's to build your life around it. To serve it. To submit your decisions to it. And in doing so, you choke out the very breath God placed in you to begin with.

Money itself isn't evil. In fact, in Hebrew (keceph, Strong's H3701), it's described as a tool, something that is meant to serve a purpose. But when the tool becomes the treasure, and the treasure becomes the thing you build your life around, you are no longer building righteously. You're building idolatry with a spreadsheet.

I had to walk away from that organization. Not because the industry was evil, but because the culture was rooted in everything opposite of the Kingdom. I couldn't stay and say, "Jesus is King" with my lips while living like He was irrelevant in my decisions. I couldn't bow to money and expect God to bless it just because I sprinkled a few scriptures on top.

To stay would have been to say with my actions: "Give us Barabbas." To stay would have been to call evil good and good evil. And I couldn't do that, not for the money, not for the optics, not for the opportunities.

Micah 6:8 says, "What does the Lord require of you? To do justly, to love mercy, and to walk humbly with your God." That word "humble" (tsana, Strong's H6800) in the Hebrew means to live carefully, modestly, submitted to God's ways. There's no room for pride there. No room for self-promotion at the expense of holiness. No room for "I'll sin now and repent later." That mindset, "I'll just ask for forgiveness", reveals a heart that hasn't truly repented. Because true repentance comes with grief. With a decision. With the boundaries and safeguards that keep us from ever returning to what God already called us out of.

And yes, it might cost you. Righteousness will cost you. But what you gain in return, peace, alignment, clarity, authority, is worth far more than what the world can offer.

You'll have to walk away from some deals. You'll have to leave some rooms. You'll have to give up some connections.

But what you'll gain is clean hands. A pure heart. And a business God can trust.

Because the truth is this: we can't build on pride and then ask God to bless it. We can't violate people in the name of profit and expect to hear "Well done, good and faithful servant." We can't quote Matthew 6:33, "Seek first the Kingdom of God and His righteousness…", and then build our lives around strategies that grieve His Spirit.

If we want what He promised, we have to build it His way. And that starts with burning the blueprint we were handed by religion, performance, and pride, and asking God for His.

RESTORING THE SACREDNESS OF YOUR ASSIGNMENT

You can always tell when someone has made their platform their god. Their eyes stay fixated on opportunity, not obedience. Their steps move in rhythm with strategy, not surrender. And their hearts? Torn, between the applause of man and the affirmation of God.

But those who walk in righteousness, those who truly know the voice of the Lord, understand something most people miss: visibility is not the goal. Obedience is. And until God says, "Now is the time," any spotlight you force yourself into will expose more than it will elevate.

There's a sacredness to your assignment. And the moment you lose that sacredness in pursuit of status, your soul begins to slip into something dangerous, something religious, performative, self-centered, and hollow. But when the Spirit leads, even hidden seasons carry glory.

I'm not telling God what to do or asking Him to elevate me. I let Him do that when He knows I'm ready. That's not just humility. That's wisdom. That's righteousness.

The Trap of Premature Promotion

Let's call it what it is: the spiritual thirst trap. It's that unspoken temptation to prove your anointing by forcing your visibility. But it's not new.

Even Jesus faced it.

In the wilderness, Satan offered Him instant elevation: "If you are the Son of God… jump. Call on the angels. Worship me, and I'll give you all this." (See Matthew 4:1-11)

Every test was an invitation to perform, prove, or promote. But Jesus didn't fall for it. He chose the slow, obedient path, the one that didn't gratify His flesh but honored His Father.

And that's what many of us are being invited into today. Not an exit from purpose, but a purification of our pursuit. To build without being baited by visibility. To serve without striving. To walk worthy of the call without prostituting the call for platforms.

This is how you restore the sacredness of your assignment: you stop trying to be seen. And you start being still.

VISIBILITY VS. OBSCURITY: DISCERN THE DIFFERENCE

You made an important distinction between being "hidden" and being "invisible." One is Spirit-led covering. The other is flesh-based rejection.

- When God hides you, He's protecting the seed.
- When people ignore you, they're rejecting the fruit.

Your job is not to change the outcome, it's to stay planted and faithful. Too many women of God are wasting energy trying to get in rooms that God never sent them to, or worse, begging for mentorship from people He never assigned to them.

But when you've restored the sacredness of your assignment, you're no longer thirsty for rooms. You're faithful in your wilderness. You're present in the field, like David. You're content building behind the scenes like Moses. And when God says "now," you don't need to perform, you just need to obey.

THE WEIGHT YOU WEREN'T BUILT TO CARRY

This is where so many falter. They push, promote, and posture their way into rooms. But once inside, the weight of premature promotion begins to crush them.

Because favor without formation is a trap. You see it everywhere: Leaders crushed by the expectations they were never built to carry. Platforms turned into prisons. Ministries derailed by ego. Businesses corrupted by greed. And at the root of it? A refusal to wait on God's timing.

That's why your approach is rare, and righteous. You said, "Some of the storms people are facing today are not attacks. They're consequences for putting themselves in positions that God never called them to."

That's the kind of wisdom the Church needs. And it's the kind of wisdom this marketplace revival is going to require. Because as God raises up Kingdom entrepreneurs, the temptation to seek the spotlight will increase.

But make no mistake: If you chase elevation without formation, it's not a blessing, it's a burden.

WHAT HAPPENS WHEN YOU LET GOD LEAD

When God is truly the One guiding your steps, a few things begin to shift:

- You stop looking at numbers and start looking at names, because you realize your assignment is always about people.
- You stop rushing the process and start receiving from the process, because you know God is using it to prepare you.
- You stop idolizing outcomes and start stewarding your obedience, because you know impact is a byproduct of intimacy.

And most of all, you stop striving for success and start sowing into the sacred. That's what restores the sacredness of your assignment. That's what keeps you pure, grounded, and unshaken when the temptations of performance and self-promotion come knocking.

And they will come.

The enemy will whisper: "You should be further by now. You should be bigger by now. You deserve more credit."

But when you've restored the sacred, you'll reply with the same confidence Jesus had in the wilderness: "I only do what I see my Father doing." (John 5:19)

HIDDEN ON PURPOSE

We don't talk about the gift of being hidden enough. In a world that rewards visibility, content output, and the constant need to be seen, it feels countercultural to say, "God told me to stay behind the scenes." But if you've ever been truly led by the Spirit, you know that hiddenness is not punishment. It's protection. It's preparation. It's proof that God cares more about your becoming than your branding.

I learned this the hard way. When I first gave my life to the Lord at sixteen, I came out of gangs, drugs, and a lifestyle that almost killed me. Literally. I had overdosed and landed in the hospital. It was there, in a moment of desperation, that God met me face-to-face and changed the trajectory of my life forever. I was radically saved and baptized with the Holy Spirit. The Word of God came alive to me. But my deliverance didn't happen overnight. I still needed renewal of the mind. I still needed healing. I still needed to unlearn everything that my old life taught me about survival, pride, and performance.

And that's exactly why God kept me hidden.

There were seasons where I wanted the platform. I wanted to teach. I wanted to preach. But the doors wouldn't open. I thought it was rejection. Now I know it was grace. Because if God would've given me what I asked for, I would've collapsed under the weight of it. Not because I didn't love Him, but because my character couldn't carry the call yet. He was still refining me.

God's mercy is often disguised as obscurity. And we have to stop treating it like exile.

The hidden season is where God matures us, fortifies us, and strips away everything that could become a counterfeit source of identity. It's where He shows us how to hear His voice, not the voice of applause. It's where He teaches us how to move with integrity when no one is watching. It's the equivalent of a fighter training for years before they ever enter the ring. No boxer gets handed a championship fight without a track record of private discipline and unseen preparation.

The same was true for Jesus. He didn't begin His public ministry until He was thirty years old, even though He had been about His Father's business since He was a boy. His hidden years were not wasted. They were sacred.

And if the Son of God wasn't rushed into public ministry, why are we trying to rush ourselves?

For me, the hidden years became the incubator where my identity was forged. I stopped seeing success as optics and started seeing it as obedience. There's a major difference between being platformed and being positioned by God. One is the result of hustle. The other is the fruit of intimacy. When you're positioned by God, He gives you influence that moves things in heaven and on earth. You don't just have visibility. You have authority. There's a deep difference between influence and authority. One gathers likes and followers. The other shifts atmospheres and overturns demonic systems. You don't need to be seen to have power. Elijah wasn't famous, but when he prayed, the heavens shut. And then they opened again. (1 Kings 17-18)

So how do I discern the difference between when God is asking me to stay hidden and when He's calling me into visibility?

I listen. And I obey. It really is that simple. God doesn't speak in riddles or vague metaphors. When He wants me to move, He gives me clarity. When He tells me to speak, I speak. When He tells me to pause, I pause. That's what being Spirit-led looks like. It's not self-promotion wrapped in religious language. It's radical submission to His voice, even when it doesn't make sense.

There have been moments when following God's instruction led me into rooms of great visibility. And there have been times when that same obedience kept me behind the curtain. But in both cases, I had peace. Because I wasn't following a career strategy. I was following the cloud.

And that's the issue. Some of us are more committed to being seen than we are to being sent.

We want visibility, but we're not willing to be purified. We want platforms, but we don't want process. We want fruit without pruning. But God loves us too much to allow us to gain influence that our character can't sustain.

I've seen firsthand what happens when people force visibility. Especially in Christian circles. Some step into positions of authority that God never called them to, and when storms come, their lack of foundation becomes clear. Others try to shortcut the process and end up producing fruit that looks good on the outside but is rotten on the inside. That's what happens when you value optics over obedience.

Let me say it like this: It is better to be hidden in obedience than exalted in disobedience.

Because elevation without preparation is sabotage. It will either expose your weaknesses or amplify your pride. Either way, it will cost you. And sometimes that cost is not just a ruined reputation. It's your soul.

As I matured in my walk, I began to see that God was protecting me from building too soon. He was saving me from premature exposure. And He was reshaping the way I define influence, visibility, and success.

That's when I wrote the following social media post:

THE TRUTH ABOUT INFLUENCE

Something has been bothering me for a while. I keep hearing Christian influencers and even preachers talk about having influence as if the measure of our effectiveness in God's Kingdom is based on numbers, crowds, and followers. They make it sound like if you are not well known, liked, or platformed, then you are not making a real impact for God.

But I have searched the scriptures, and I cannot find anything to support this. In fact, I see the complete opposite.

INFLUENCE IN THE KINGDOM IS NOT ABOUT POPULARITY

If influence were about numbers, then by that logic, the most powerful people in God's Kingdom would be celebrities, mega pastors, and social media influencers. But when I look at the Bible, I see that some of the most powerful, anointed, and truly effective people had little to no crowd support. Some were even rejected and despised.

- Noah was a righteous man, but out of the entire world, only his family listened to him. (Genesis 6-9)

- Jeremiah spoke God's words, but he was persecuted, beaten, and imprisoned because people did not like what he had to say. (Jeremiah 20:1-2)
- John the Baptist prepared the way for Jesus, yet he ended up in prison and was executed. (Matthew 14:1-12)
- Jesus Himself had thousands follow Him at one point, but when He started preaching hard truths, many abandoned Him. (John 6:66)

Nowhere does the Bible say that effectiveness is tied to public approval. If anything, it warns that the world will reject those who follow Christ wholeheartedly.

> *"WHAT SORROW AWAITS YOU WHO ARE PRAISED BY THE CROWDS, FOR THEIR ANCESTORS ALSO PRAISED FALSE PROPHETS." (LUKE 6:26, NLT)*

TRUE KINGDOM INFLUENCE IS SPIRITUAL, NOT SOCIAL

In God's Kingdom, real influence comes from intimacy with God, obedience, and humility. It never comes from popularity. If heaven does not recognize your authority, then having thousands of people follow you means absolutely nothing. The Bible makes it clear that spiritual power comes from a life of humility, submission, and prayer. It never comes from having an audience.

> "HUMBLE YOURSELVES BEFORE THE LORD, AND HE WILL LIFT YOU UP IN HONOR." (JAMES 4:10, NLT)

> "BUT WHEN YOU PRAY, GO AWAY BY YOURSELF, SHUT THE DOOR BEHIND YOU, AND PRAY TO YOUR FATHER IN PRIVATE. THEN YOUR FATHER, WHO SEES EVERYTHING,

> *WILL REWARD YOU." (MATTHEW 6:6, NLT)*

> *"THEN IF MY PEOPLE WHO ARE CALLED BY MY NAME WILL HUMBLE THEMSELVES AND PRAY AND SEEK MY FACE AND TURN FROM THEIR WICKED WAYS, I WILL HEAR FROM HEAVEN AND WILL FORGIVE THEIR SINS AND RESTORE THEIR LAND." (2 CHRONICLES 7:14, NLT)*

Did you catch that? It is God who moves on behalf of those who are submitted to Him, not on behalf of those with a massive following.

GOD'S POWER MOVES THROUGH THE HUMBLE, NOT THE FAMOUS

Jesus made it clear that greatness in the Kingdom is not about who is seen but who serves.

> *"BUT AMONG YOU IT WILL BE DIFFERENT. WHOEVER WANTS TO BE A LEADER AMONG YOU MUST BE YOUR SERVANT, AND WHOEVER WANTS TO BE FIRST AMONG YOU MUST BECOME YOUR SLAVE."*
> *(MATTHEW 20:26-27, NLT)*

Paul reinforced this truth:

> *"YOU MUST HAVE THE SAME ATTITUDE THAT CHRIST JESUS HAD. THOUGH HE WAS GOD, HE DID NOT THINK OF EQUALITY WITH GOD AS SOMETHING TO CLING TO. INSTEAD, HE GAVE UP HIS DIVINE PRIVILEGES. HE TOOK THE HUMBLE POSITION OF A SLAVE AND WAS BORN AS A HUMAN BEING."*
> *(PHILIPPIANS 2:5-7, NLT)*

THE BOTTOM LINE

The modern obsession with being an influencer in the Christian space is not biblical. God never called us to chase platforms. He called us to chase Him.

True influence, the kind that moves heaven, comes from submission, prayer, and obedience. It never comes from having a fanbase.

If you are seeking to be used by God, do not look at numbers. Look at your heart. If the only people you ever influence are the ones in your home, your workplace, or your church, that is enough. God sees.

And if He wants to elevate you, He will do it in His way and in His timing. But let's not get it twisted. Having a following does not mean you are powerful. Being known in heaven does.

THE DEATH OF YOUR WILL IS THE BIRTHPLACE OF POWER

Surrender sounds romantic until it costs you everything you wanted. And the truth is, it will.

Your image. Your success. Your pace. Your plans. Your connections. Your comfort. At some point, God will ask for all of it. Not to ruin you. But to resurrect you.

Because the truth is, the resurrection always requires a death.

For me, the death of my will didn't come in a single altar moment. It came in layers. It came through confrontation. Conviction. And a quiet, internal breaking that no one else could see. I had to admit that what I wanted was different from what God was asking for. And I had to choose: obedience or outcome.

The hardest part? I knew His will would cost me.

It meant closing down my brick-and-mortar store even though it was successful. It meant letting go of income and reputation tied to the insurance industry because the leaders I once trusted chose unethical paths. It meant walking away from residuals, prestige, and open doors, all because God whispered, "Choose Me."

And make no mistake, obedience cost me in the short-term.

But disobedience would have cost me everything.

I would not be alive, healthy, or whole if I had clung to the momentum I built in my own strength. That's the difference between striving and surrender. One exhausts your body and drains your soul. The other saves it.

I had to learn that comfort and calling rarely go together.

We've been conditioned to believe that the gospel guarantees ease. But Jesus never promised that. He promised peace, not comfort. He promised persecution, process, and power. Not platforms.

He didn't come to make our lives easier. He came to make our lives eternal.

So when He says "Die to yourself," He doesn't mean become irrelevant. He means become unshakable.

WHEN GOD ASKS FOR YOUR WILL

One of the biggest patterns God broke in me was the fear of what people would think. I was so bound by optics. So trained to make decisions based on how it would look. But God had to teach me that faith isn't about looking strong. It's about being surrendered.

There's a kind of pride that creeps in when you're building something in public. You start protecting your "momentum" more than you protect your heart. You start caring more about how it appears than whether God is still in it.

And then there's people-pleasing. That sneaky little pattern that makes you say yes to others when God already told you no. That part of your soul that doesn't want to disappoint anyone, even if it means disappointing God.

I had to confront all of it. Not in a big dramatic way. But in the private, daily decisions. The moments when I had to go back to someone and say, "I know I said yes. But I have to follow God. And the answer is no."

That takes maturity. That takes courage. That takes dying to your ego.

But the moment you die to the pressure of being understood, you come alive in the power of being obedient.

WHAT DEATH UNLOCKS

The moment I let go of my will, God began to unlock levels of wisdom, insight, and strategy that I never had access to before. Where I once had ideas with no clarity, I suddenly had framework. Where I once worked tirelessly to figure things out, I now had divine downloads that put all the pieces together.

That's what Jesus meant when He said, "My yoke is easy, and my burden is light." (Matthew 11:30) He didn't mean there wouldn't be weight. He meant His weight doesn't crush you. It carries you.

DYING TO YOURSELF DOESN'T MEAN LIVING SMALL. IT MEANS LIVING HOLY.

It means the more you let go of control, the more clearly you begin to see what God has been trying to show you all along. Your business stops being a machine you're building, and starts becoming a message He's breathing.

Your life becomes weighty. Precise. Prophetic. You start getting insight into your industry and your assignment that can't be Googled or copied. That's divine authority. And it can only be accessed through surrender.

People may be able to imitate your branding. But they'll never be able to duplicate your blueprint, because the blueprint was downloaded in the hidden place. It was birthed in death.

IF YOU'RE STILL HESITATING, READ THIS AGAIN

If you're afraid of surrendering, let me go ahead and tell you the truth up front: it will cost you.
It will cost you your version of momentum. But that momentum takes years to build and a lifetime to maintain. God's momentum can change everything in a single moment. One yes can do what your hustle never could.
It will cost you your version of success. But your version of success will burn you out. God's success builds legacy without

compromising your soul. It multiplies your fruit without bankrupting your peace.

It will cost you your image. But your image was never the point. Look at Joseph. No PR strategy could've protected him when Potiphar's wife falsely accused him. But God didn't just protect Joseph, He promoted him. In one day, Joseph went from prisoner to palace. You don't need to control the narrative when God is the One writing your story.

And yes, it may cost you some relationships. But some of those relationships are the reason your mind has been stuck. They're the reason you haven't healed. Because you can't heal in the same environment that broke you. You're not letting go of people. You're letting go of the spirit that's been using them to keep you bound.

Because here's the enemy's strategy: if he can keep you afraid of surrender, he can keep you enslaved.

But when you die to your will, you finally rise in His.

And that is the birthplace of power.

LET GO OF THE LIE, GRAB HOLD OF THE LIGHT

Sweetheart, I know you've been trying to hold onto this image for the longest time. You've been performing. You've been posturing. You've been running hard, not just to prove you're righteous, but to prove you're worthy.

Worthy of love. Worthy of success. Worthy of being taken seriously.

Maybe you've been trying to prove to the people who judged you in the past. Maybe you're chasing success just to silence that voice in your head that keeps calling you dumb, unqualified, or not good enough. Maybe you're trying to prove you're not the same girl you used to be.

And the truth is... you're exhausted.

You feel like you're running on a hamster wheel. You're building, pushing, striving, but deep down, nothing feels steady. Nothing feels like it's working in your favor. The more you perform, the more disconnected you feel from your own soul. So let me ask you gently, but boldly: Are you ready to let go?

Because here's the truth: If you're tired of holding it all together, it's not weakness, it's a signal. A holy signal. One that says it's time to surrender. It's time to stop chasing and start trusting. It's time to stop building based on pressure and start building based on peace.

It's time to let God define what success looks like for your life, not Instagram. Not your old church. Not your childhood trauma. Not the business guru who doesn't know your name.

And here's what I can promise you:

Letting go will cost you.

Dying to yourself won't feel easy.

Surrendering the lies that have lived in your head for decades will feel like tearing bricks out of your own foundation.

But once you let go of the lie, you make room to grab hold of the light.

The lie told you that performance earns love. That achievement proves value. That success is the same thing as freedom. But none of that is true.

Because what your soul really craves is not just to be impressive. It's to be free. Free to create without compromise. Free to rest without guilt. Free to obey God without overthinking how people will perceive it. Free to wake up and love the life you've been assigned. Free to be still. Free to be known. Free to be held.

And that kind of freedom doesn't come from hustle.

It comes from surrender.

So let this be your moment. Let this be your pivot.

You've done enough pretending. You've carried enough pressure. You've said yes to enough of the wrong things. This is your permission to breathe again.

Let go of the lie. Grab hold of the light.

And let God lead you into the kind of life you no longer have to perform to keep.

CHAPTER 3

THE LIE OF THE INDUSTRY STANDARD

WHEN YOU BUILD *WITH* GOD, YOU DON'T HAVE TO PROVE ANYTHING

We quote that scripture all the time in church circles, about building on the rock instead of the sand so that what we build can withstand the testing of time. But I didn't fully understand that verse until I learned the difference between building with God and building for God.

Building for God may sound noble, but it's rooted in a faulty mindset. It's driven by a quiet but toxic belief that we have something to prove, that we owe God something we can never repay. We hustle to earn our place, our worth, our belonging. We convince ourselves that we're "doing it for the Kingdom" or "for our family," but deep down we're still striving, desperate to prove we deserve love, honor, or value.

It's the same orphan mindset that tells you love is earned and worth is achieved.

But building with God is completely different. It's not transactional, it's relational.

When you build with God, you're not trying to earn His favor. You're responding to His

presence. You're not striving to meet industry standards. You're stewarding Heaven's blueprint. You're not trying to "pay Him back." You're simply saying yes to what He's already authored.
It becomes a dance of delight.

> "DELIGHT YOURSELF IN THE LORD, AND HE WILL GIVE YOU THE DESIRES OF YOUR HEART."
> (PSALM 37:4, NLT)

That verse isn't about getting everything we want. It's about becoming so rooted in God that our desires become aligned with His. And when our desires are His desires, He responds with power. He opens the doors. He provides the strategy. He sends the resources. He builds it with you.
Will there still be hard days? Of course. But you won't be building alone. Heaven

will back you. His Spirit will sustain you. His peace will protect you. And His favor will follow you, not because you earned it, but because you walk with Him.

That's the real difference. When you build with God, you're no longer just a servant of God. You're His daughter. And as you grow in intimacy and obedience, you move into friendship with God.

That's not just business. That's Kingdom.

THE BUSINESS PLAN THAT BREAKS THE RULES

Why Kingdom Builders Don't Fit the Mold, And Aren't Supposed To

This isn't coming from a mountaintop. I'm not writing this from a place of having it all figured out. This is mid-process, mid-surrender, mid-revelation. I'm not giving you a formula to follow. I'm sharing a conversation between me and God that you've been invited into, because this message is shaping me just as much as it's meant to shape you.

Let me tell you why kingdom builders never quite fit the mold.

We don't start with plans.

We start with presence.

We don't chase blueprints.

We chase the face of God.

Every God-ordained business begins in the secret place, not in a strategy session. The boardroom doesn't come before the prayer room. Intimacy with God is not something we do after the LLC papers are signed or after we hit our first six figures. It's the foundation before anything gets built.

That's the first rule we break,

The world says: "Start with a business

plan."

But the Kingdom says: "Start with Me you God."

In that place of fasting, prayer, and quiet communion with God, you don't just get business ideas. You get God's heart. You stop asking Him to bless your plan and start asking Him to reveal His. That shift changes everything.

You don't walk out of that place with a 10-step launch calendar.

You walk out marked, with discernment, with direction, and with the kind of peace that makes no sense given the pressure you're under.

Because let's be real.

Business will test you.

It will trigger your fears.

It will stretch your faith.

And on some days, it will tempt you to question everything you've built.

But if your foundation is intimacy, not image, if your blueprint is obedience, not outcome, you'll weather it. You'll listen differently. Move differently. Build differently.

The industry says you need to post 10 times a day, run 6 ads, launch 4 funnels, write daily emails, be on TikTok, go viral, and constantly chase visibility.

God says:

Come sit with Me first.

Listen.

Move when I say move.

Speak when I say speak.

That doesn't mean you don't do your due diligence. It doesn't mean you don't have structure, strategy, or stewardship. But your first responsibility is not to hustle harder. It's to hear clearer.

This kind of business plan is disruptive.

It will not always make sense.

It will not always follow trends.

But it will always bear fruit.

Because you're not guessing anymore.

You're not grinding for survival.

You're flowing from spiritual clarity.

This is what makes us different. This is what gives us an unfair advantage.

We have access to insider information, the kind only the Holy Spirit can reveal.

And that's the power of building a business that breaks the rules.

THE PSYCHOLOGY OF WHY WE CLING TO "STANDARDS"

Not every industry standard is a trap. Some exist to protect people. When I ran my skincare company, there were requirements I needed to follow. Proper labels. Accurate ingredient lists. Safety disclosures. Those are not optional if you plan to honor the law and the people you serve. Order is godly. Stewardship is righteous. Excellence is not rebellion.

But there is a different kind of standard. The kind everyone follows because it is common, not because it is clean. The kind the market normalizes because it is profitable, not because it is pure. This is where a believer must slow down, seek God, and test everything.

Here is what that looked like for me. I would research an ingredient that the industry considered safe. The label said it passed. The regulations said it passed. Yet when I dug into academic journals and patterns of real world experience, I saw enough red flags to make me pause. Lobbying was loud. Money was moving. Adverse effects were surfacing. The law allowed it, but my spirit did not. So I chose a different path. I honored the law without violating conscience. I found alternatives that served the body the way God designed it to function. I refused to trade health for margins.

This is the heart of the matter. Just because everybody is doing it does not make it righteous. You have access to a better source. God's wisdom is not limited by trends or trade groups. Ask Him for the formula. Ask Him for the timing. Ask Him for the path that obeys the law without bowing to what is unclean.

So why do we still cling to the mold when we know better? Underneath the surface, several forces are at work.

Fear of failure. We copy what is common because we believe it will reduce the risk of loss. If it worked for them, maybe it will work for me. Fear masquerades as prudence.

Comparison and imposter syndrome. We elevate loud experts and minimize the voice of the Spirit. We forget that influence does not equal authority. We forget that followers do not equal fruit.

Underdeveloped discernment. We have not trained our ear to recognize God's voice in the noise. Instead of weighing counsel before God, we outsource conviction to algorithms and audiences.

Reward learning. When a questionable tactic produces fast results, our brain tags it as useful. Short term reward rewires conscience if we do not interrupt the pattern with truth.

Image management. We fear being seen as naive or unprofessional if we break from the norm. We protect perception instead of protecting people.

The fix is not rejection of all standards. The fix is consecration. Weigh it all before God. Ask better questions.

Is it legal, but is it ethical.

Is it ethical, but is it righteous.

Is it profitable, but is it pure.

Will it scale, but will it stain.

Scripture gives us a way forward. God invites us to ask for wisdom and promises to give it generously without rebuke (James 1:5). He tells us to test everything and hold on to what is good (1 Thessalonians 5:21). He calls us to refuse the squeeze of this world's patterns and to be transformed by renewing the mind so we can learn His will, which is good, pleasing, and perfect (Romans 12:2). When counsel conflicts with conviction, we obey God rather than men (Acts 5:29). That is not arrogance. That is alignment. Here is the shift. Excellence in the Kingdom is not blind conformity. It is informed obedience. It is the courage to keep what protects people and discard what pollutes them. It is the humility to learn from experts and the boldness to submit every expert to the Spirit of Truth. It is the willingness to walk the slower path if the faster one would cost you your integrity.

This is the psychology behind clean business. You retrain your reflex from panic to prayer. You move from copy and compete to listen and obey. You replace the fear of missing out with the fear of the Lord. You stop asking, "Will this make me look credible" and start asking, "Will this make me more faithful." And when you build like that, you will sleep at night. You will look people in the eye. You will produce solutions that do not quietly harm the people they promise to help. You will become a builder God can trust.

DISCERNMENT IN STRATEGY

Excellence without discernment is just performance.

Strategy without surrender is still self-reliance.

That's where many high-capacity believers get stuck, we're gifted, skilled, and strategic, but we start leaning on the system that once oppressed us.

You can have the best marketing plan in the world, the sharpest copy, and the most polished brand, but if your decisions are not filtered through the Spirit of God, you'll still end up exhausted, anxious, and spiritually bankrupt. Because Kingdom strategy isn't just about what works; it's about what's right.

The world says, "Data doesn't lie."

Heaven says, "Truth doesn't change."

And those two statements are not the same.

The Holy Spirit will sometimes lead you into a launch that makes no sense on paper but is perfectly aligned with Heaven's timing. He will also tell you not to launch something that looks profitable if it will wound your witness. Strategy, in the Kingdom, begins with reverence.

That means before you adopt a system, ask if it serves the mission.

Before you mimic a method, ask if it honors your mantle.

Before you copy a standard, ask if it aligns with Scripture.

God's strategies will always require trust. He will test whether you value alignment over applause. Sometimes, He'll let you stay hidden because exposure too early would corrupt what He's forming in you. Other times, He'll call you to step forward when you feel unqualified, to prove that obedience outranks expertise.

Discernment in strategy looks like this:

You plan, but you also pause.

You measure, but you also meditate.

You build, but you also break when God says to pivot.

You listen to mentors, but you weigh their words against the Word.

That's not passivity, it's maturity. It's the ability to lead with peace instead of pressure. Because when your business is built with God, not just for Him, every plan becomes a partnership.

Excellence, then, is not perfectionism. It's consecration. It's doing your best work with a clean heart, free hands, and pure motives. It's honoring both natural wisdom and supernatural guidance. It's knowing that order pleases God, but manipulation never does.

That's the kind of excellence that breaks the lie of the industry standard.

It's not about outperforming others, it's about out-obeying fear.

Dig Deeper

1. Where am I following industry standards out of fear instead of faith?
2. What systems or strategies have I accepted as "normal" that the Holy Spirit has quietly convicted me to question?
3. Have I confused excellence with perfectionism? How can I bring my focus back to obedience instead of optics?
4. In what areas do I need to invite God back into my strategy before I take another step?
5. What would change if I stopped chasing what's common and started protecting what's qadash, set apart for Him?

Righteousness in the Marketplace

PART II - REFINING THE BUILDER

CHAPTER 4

WHAT INTEGRITY COSTS (AND WHAT IT'S WORTH)

WHEN DOING THE RIGHT THING MAKES YOU LOOK LIKE THE PROBLEM

Some people think integrity means keeping the peace. But if you study your Bible, you'll see that godly integrity often disrupted the peace, especially when that "peace" was built on corruption, compromise, or fear.

Let's get something straight: integrity doesn't mean playing it safe. It means doing what's right even when it's politically dangerous, personally costly, and publicly misunderstood.

Look at John the Baptist.

Herod took his brother's wife. Everyone knew it was wrong, but no one said a word, except John. He didn't tiptoe around it. He called it out, publicly and directly. And it cost him everything. His platform. His freedom. His life.

Now pause and look at what Jesus did later.

During His own trial, Jesus was brought before the same man who had John executed. And Jesus, who had no problem calling out Pharisees or flipping temple tables, said absolutely nothing to Herod. Silence. Not out of fear, but out of judgment. It was as if heaven refused to dignify the presence of a man who silenced a prophet. That silence honored John's courage. And it exposed Herod's guilt.

Now zoom out.

The apostles were warned by the Sanhedrin to stop preaching. These were the men with power to jail them or worse. But they didn't soften their message. They didn't hide behind polite language. They said, "We must obey God rather than human beings" (Acts 5:29). That wasn't rebellion. That was submission to a higher authority. That was integrity in real time. And here's the part we don't like to admit in church circles: doing the right thing won't always make you look righteous. Sometimes it'll make you look difficult.

Disruptive. Rebellious. Even dishonorable, especially to people who benefit from your silence.

We've learned how to use "wisdom" as camouflage for fear. We've gotten really good at calling it "discernment" when it's really self-preservation. And all the while, injustice spreads under our so-called "neutrality."

But here's the truth: integrity has a cost. And if you haven't felt it yet, you're not as bold as you think you are.

Integrity is not just about how you do business. It's about whether or not your life confronts the darkness around you. It's about whether your silence protects your reputation or reflects God's heart.

This section of the chapter is not here to shame you. It's here to wake you up.

Because if you're building something in

this world, whether it's a business, a family, or a legacy, you will be tempted to trade truth for approval. You will be pressured to stay quiet so you can stay connected. And you will be labeled "too much" or "too intense" or "too self-righteous" the moment you start taking integrity seriously.

But that's when you know you're doing it right.

Because righteousness rarely gets applause in real time. It gets questioned. It gets mocked. And sometimes, it gets crucified.

But heaven sees.

And if you're willing to walk through the fire of being misunderstood, God will trust you with a legacy that can't be manipulated.

WHEN HUSTLING BECOMES A FALSE GOD

It's easy to say we trust God with our business, but the truth shows up in the way we carry pressure.

There's a kind of pride that doesn't announce itself with arrogance, it disguises itself as responsibility. It looks like being the go-to person for everything. It sounds like, "If I don't do it, it won't get done." It feels like that weight in your chest at 2 AM because your brain won't stop calculating everything that could go wrong.

And the worst part? It works. For a while. You hit goals. You impress people. You build systems. You gain momentum.

But instead of feeling full, you start to feel fractured.

That's the trap of performance-based living. It leads you to believe that success depends entirely on your effort, your skill, your grind, and it feeds a dangerous lie: This is all on me.

And it was. Because when God is not invited to be your partner, your source, and your strategist, He lets you run the show, but He also lets you carry the weight. He'll let you see what your hands can build without Him, and how quickly it can fall when they get tired.

That kind of success becomes a self-constructed prison.

You can't slow down. You can't breathe. You can't trust anyone else to help. And soon, you're not just disconnected from God, you're disconnected from people. Pride starts whispering that you're the exception. That no one works like you.

That no one understands your burden.
That no one else is trustworthy enough to carry the weight with you.

It's the same pride that whispered to Nebuchadnezzar as he looked over Babylon and declared, "Look at this great city I have built by my own mighty power" (Daniel 4:30). That kind of thinking didn't just lead to anxiety, it led to insanity. Because when we worship the hustle instead of the One who gives us the ability to build, we're no longer operating in Kingdom alignment, we're serving a false god.

Moses warned Israel about this trap:

> *"HE DID ALL THIS SO YOU WOULD NEVER SAY TO YOURSELF, 'I HAVE ACHIEVED THIS WEALTH WITH MY OWN STRENGTH AND ENERGY.' REMEMBER THE LORD YOUR GOD. HE IS THE ONE WHO GIVES YOU*

*POWER TO BE SUCCESSFUL."
(DEUTERONOMY 8:17–18, NLT)*

And that power isn't just about income, it's about insight. It's the power to know what to build, when to build, and how to build it in a way that doesn't bankrupt your soul. God never asked you to carry the pressure of Babylon.

He called you to partner with Heaven.

IF YOU'RE STILL HESITATING, READ THIS AGAIN

Sweetheart, I know you've been trying to hold onto this image for the longest time. You've been performing. You've been running hard to prove yourself, not only to prove that you're righteous, but to prove that you're worthy. To prove that you've got the skills, that you've got what it takes.

Maybe even to prove to the people in the past who judged you and said you wouldn't amount to anything, that you would. That you beat the odds. That you won.

You've been trying to prove something to the voice inside your head that says you're stupid, you're not good enough, you're not capable. And everything in you has been trying to shout back, "Yes, I am."

There's all these reasons why we do what we do. Why we hang on to the ideas and the paths and the thoughts of what we thought it could be.

But if you're tired of performing, if you're emotionally and spiritually exhausted, like you're running in a hamster wheel and no matter how hard you work, nothing seems to move forward, then maybe it's time to surrender.

It's time to let go. To let God lead. To let Him define what success looks like in your life instead of you clinging to a definition that's draining the life out of you.

And I promise you: it will be worth it.

Will the road be easy? Absolutely not. Dying to self is never easy. Surrendering to God and letting go of the lies that have been embedded in your heart for decades is not easy. Those lies became familiar. They became your version of "truth." But those lies were planted by the enemy to keep you bound.

If you don't surrender, if you don't allow God to guide you and show you what His version of success looks like, you will never taste true freedom.

And I love you too much not to tell you this: What your soul is craving is not success. It's freedom.

Freedom to be who you are. Freedom to create freely. Freedom to wake up excited about the life you're living. Freedom for your soul to finally breathe.

And that kind of freedom? It only comes through surrender.

THE SPIRIT OF BABYLON STILL BUILDS

Babylon is not just an ancient city, it's a spirit. A system. A counterfeit kingdom built on the illusion of power, the seduction of wealth, and the worship of human strength.

In the Bible, Babylon was known for its towering achievements, its advanced systems, and its visible success. But it was also the place that tried to build without God.

> *"COME, LET'S BUILD A GREAT CITY FOR OURSELVES WITH A TOWER THAT REACHES INTO THE SKY. THIS WILL MAKE US FAMOUS..."*
> *(GENESIS 11:4, NLT)*

Babylon says:

- Build fast.
- Build high.
- Build for your name.

But the Kingdom says:

- Build sustainable.
- Build deep.
- Build for God's glory.

Babylon exalts human will. The Kingdom bows to God's will.

This is why Babylon will always feel urgent, exhausting, and heavy, it has no rest. No Sabbath. No altar.

Just noise. Hustle. Pressure.

> *"SHE GLORIFIED HERSELF AND LIVED IN LUXURY, SO MATCH IT NOW WITH TORMENT AND SORROW. SHE BOASTED IN HER HEART, 'I AM QUEEN ON MY THRONE. I AM NO HELPLESS WIDOW, AND I HAVE NO REASON TO MOURN.'"*
> *(REVELATION 18:7, NLT)*

But when God says "Come out of her," He's not just talking about a physical location. He's calling His people to abandon the mindset of self-made striving.

You don't have to build Babylon.

You were made to build what Heaven can bless.

Dig Deeper

1. Where in my life have I mistaken keeping the peace for keeping integrity?

2. Have I ever softened my conviction or stayed silent to protect relationships, opportunities, or reputation?

3. What does it currently cost me to live with integrity, and have I been resenting that cost or honoring it as worship?
4. In what areas of my work or leadership have I carried pressure God never asked me to carry?
5. Have I made the hustle an idol? How can I shift from striving for outcomes to partnering with God in obedience?
6. What would my business, ministry, or leadership look like if I truly believed that freedom, not success, is the goal?
7. What would "coming out of Babylon" look like in my daily rhythms, my schedule, my conversations, my decisions, and my rest?

Righteousness in the Marketplace

CHAPTER 5

RIGHTEOUSNESS ISN'T A MARKETING STRATEGY

"GOD FIRST" ISN'T A GIMMICK

I get frustrated when I see people using phrases like "God first" or "kingdom business" as a marketing angle, but their methods don't reflect the integrity that those words are supposed to carry. I'm not saying that from a place of judgment. I'm saying it from a place of deep grief and discernment. Because when you really live by those words, it changes how you operate, down to the smallest detail.

Let me tell you about a moment that really brought this home.

There was a product I used to love back in my teenage years, a supplement I found helpful and genuinely beneficial. When I saw it re-emerge on the market recently, I thought, Okay, let me try it again and maybe even share it with others. There was nothing wrong with the product itself. In fact, I still don't have a single bad thing to say about it.

The issue came with the people responsible for providing the business training.

This particular group identified as believers. The leaders were people of integrity, men and women of God, no issues there. But the trainers I was assigned to? That's where the problem was. They started pushing methods that were completely out of alignment with the character and heart of God. They coached me to use manipulative tactics. They literally recommended guilt-based language to get people to buy the product or join the business. And because they wrapped it in "kingdom" language, they tried to make it sound holy.

But let's be clear: guilt wrapped in scripture is still manipulation. And manipulation, especially when done in God's name, isn't just unethical. It's demonic.

We don't use God to get what we want from people. We don't coerce others into thinking that buying from us or joining our business is somehow "kingdom alignment" while painting their no as spiritual disobedience.

THAT'S NOT BIBLICAL. THAT'S NOT RIGHTEOUS. THAT'S WITCHCRAFT.

Yes, I said it. Witchcraft.
Because what else do you call it when someone uses spiritual language to override another person's agency? When they quote scripture to create false obligation? When they exploit your desire to honor God as a tactic to make a sale? We don't see that anywhere in scripture. The only way Jesus ever judged whether someone was putting God first was by

looking at the posture of their heart and their obedience, not by whether or not they bought from someone in ministry. Yes, we will know people by their fruit. But fruit isn't forced. Fruit is cultivated over time. And no matter how much we think we know someone's heart, the truth is, we don't. Only God does.

That's why we have to be vigilant when people start twisting scripture into sales copy. That's not kingdom. That's not righteousness. That's spiritual abuse. And if this were Old Testament times, those who practiced that kind of deceit would've been dragged outside the camp and stoned, publicly. Not because God is cruel, but because He takes the misuse of His name seriously. He wanted it to be a warning: This will not be done again among My people.

Thank God for grace. Thank God we're not getting stoned today.

BUT JUST BECAUSE THERE'S GRACE DOESN'T MEAN WE TOLERATE THIS MESS.

Kingdom business is built on clean hands and a pure heart, not religious language and strategic guilt. And the moment we start using spiritual words to manipulate people into saying yes, we've crossed a line. That's not "God first." That's self first. And I refuse to build like that.

RECOGNIZING MANIPULATION IN THE NAME OF STRATEGY

There's a subtle but dangerous shift happening in the way business, especially in network marketing and personal branding, is being taught. The line between persuasion and manipulation has been trampled in the name of success. And if we're not discerning, we'll start repeating tactics that work without ever asking if they're righteous.

Let's be real: people are tired of being sold to. But more than that, they're tired of being manipulated, especially by Christians who claim to be doing business God's way while using tactics the world perfected in the shadows.

MANIPULATION MASQUERADING AS MOTIVATION

Manipulation often disguises itself in motivational language:
"Only winners will recognize this opportunity. Are you one of them?"

"Imagine quitting your job and making six figures in six months. Don't you want that kind of freedom?"

These phrases don't inspire, they pressure. They prey on fear of missing out and challenge someone's identity by suggesting that to say no is to fail.

You've probably heard them in network marketing. But they're everywhere, in coaching, course sales, business masterminds, and even ministry circles. They create an atmosphere where the decision to walk away feels like a moral failure rather than a thoughtful choice. This is not kingdom.

GOD'S STANDARD: INTEGRITY IN EVERY INTERACTION

Let's bring this back to the Word. Proverbs 11:1 says,

> *"A FALSE BALANCE IS AN ABOMINATION TO THE LORD, BUT A JUST WEIGHT IS HIS DELIGHT."*

In business terms, that means inflated promises, emotional pressure, and manipulative hype are not just unethical, they're offensive to God.

Philippians 2:3 tells us to

> *"DO NOTHING OUT OF SELFISH AMBITION OR VAIN CONCEIT. RATHER, IN HUMILITY VALUE OTHERS ABOVE YOURSELVES."*

That's not just a verse about church life, it's a blueprint for how we engage with people in every setting, including business. Manipulation violates both of these commands. It doesn't honor the person in front of you, it exploits their hopes, fears, and insecurities to make a sale or recruit a downline.

That's not excellence. That's exploitation.

How to Tell the Difference

So what separates ethical persuasion from manipulation? Here's a clear breakdown:

Ethical Persuasion:
- Offers clear, honest information
- Respects the person's agency and timeline
- Focuses on serving, not closing

Manipulation:
- Uses shame or fear to provoke urgency
- Over-promises and under-discloses risk

- Frames disagreement or hesitation as weakness or disobedience

It's not about tone, it's about intention. And the Lord weighs the heart.

THE COST OF PRESSURE-DRIVEN CULTURE

If you have to emotionally pressure someone into buying, signing, or enrolling, you're not building a business. You're building an empire of codependency. One that will crumble the moment someone wakes up and realizes they were coerced, not served.

You don't need to shame people into saying yes. If your offer is aligned, if your service is valuable, and if your communication is clean, there will be fruit. And that fruit will remain.

As Galatians 6:7 reminds us:

> "DO NOT BE DECEIVED: GOD CANNOT BE MOCKED. A MAN REAPS WHAT HE SOWS."

If you sow pressure and fear, don't be surprised when your business is built on churn, burnout, and shallow trust.
But if you sow with integrity? You'll reap loyalty, respect, and long-term impact. That's what God can bless.

BUILD WHAT WON'T ROT

The world teaches us to hook people emotionally, close them quickly, and scale at all costs. But righteousness teaches us to **speak with clarity, serve with excellence, and let the Spirit lead.**

You can be persuasive without being manipulative. You can be excellent without being exploitative. And you can be strategic without becoming sneaky.

So if you've used manipulative tactics in the past, repent. Don't spiritualize it. Don't excuse it. Just realign.

And if you've felt uncomfortable watching others do it, trust that discomfort. That's the Spirit guarding your conscience.

Let your words reflect His heart. Let your offers respect people's dignity. Let your strategy be clean enough to lay at His feet. Because at the end of the day, your character is your conversion rate. And no marketing plan can replace the favor of God.

MINISTRY IS NOT A FUNNEL

There's a growing trend that needs to be named clearly and confronted head-on. More and more ministers, whether they identify as pastors, prophets, or apostles, are merging their spiritual authority with their entrepreneurial ventures in ways that confuse, manipulate, and monetize the very people they were called to serve. Let's be clear: there is nothing wrong with a minister having a business. Paul made tents. Lydia dealt in purple cloth. Proverbs 31 praises a woman whose hands are in both ministry and market. The problem is not business. The problem is the blurring of sacred lines.

These leaders don't start out by selling a product. They start out by releasing a "word." They claim divine revelation. They post prophetic-sounding videos and warnings. They stir spiritual urgency and emotional intensity. Then, weeks later, the pattern unfolds:

Suddenly there's a course. A program. A mid-ticket to high-ticket offering. A webinar to funnel the fear into a sale.

And all of it is now "confirmed by God."

BUT HERE'S THE QUESTION NO ONE WANTS TO ASK: WAS THE MESSAGE REALLY PROPHETIC, OR WAS IT THE PRE-LAUNCH CONTENT PLAN?

Because when you use a divine message to build trust, stir urgency, and create an atmosphere of fear and dependency, only to later introduce a paid offer, you are not leading people prophetically. You're leading them psychologically. And that matters.

Even if you disclose that there's an offer coming, if your entire communication strategy is built around using spiritual authority to drive conversion, it's still manipulation. Clarity about monetization does not justify spiritual exploitation.

THE PSYCHOLOGY BEHIND IT

What's happening here is called authority anchoring. It's when someone builds trust through spiritual or positional authority, then pivots that trust into influence over purchasing decisions.

It also includes emotional hijacking, using spiritual language to trigger fear, scarcity, urgency, or the fear of missing God. These are classic tactics used in high-conversion marketing, but when paired with prophetic language, they confuse people's discernment and override critical thinking.

People stop asking, "Do I need this?" and start asking, "Will I miss God if I don't buy this?"

THAT'S NOT A STRATEGY. THAT'S SPIRITUAL COERCION.

Scripture Is Not Silent

> *MICAH 3:11 (NLT): "YOU RULERS MAKE DECISIONS BASED ON BRIBES; YOU PRIESTS TEACH GOD'S LAWS ONLY FOR A PRICE; YOU PROPHETS WON'T PROPHESY UNLESS YOU ARE PAID. YET ALL OF YOU CLAIM TO DEPEND ON THE LORD."*

> *1 PETER 5:2: "CARE FOR THE FLOCK THAT GOD HAS ENTRUSTED TO YOU. WATCH OVER IT WILLINGLY, NOT GRUDGINGLY, NOT FOR WHAT YOU WILL GET OUT OF IT, BUT BECAUSE YOU ARE EAGER TO SERVE GOD."*

> **2 CORINTHIANS 2:17 (NLT):** *"WE ARE NOT LIKE THE MANY HUCKSTERS WHO PREACH FOR PERSONAL PROFIT. WE PREACH THE WORD OF GOD WITH SINCERITY..."*

These verses are not antiquated. They are timeless indictments against using sacred trust for self-promotion and profit.

You Can Do Both, But You Must Do It Right

Again: business isn't the problem. Monetization isn't the sin. But when you co-manage your calling and your commerce without clarity, you create a confusing hybrid that manipulates instead of ministers.

If God called you to business, do it boldly. Use your gifts. Build your products. Teach your frameworks. But don't disguise a launch strategy as a prophetic warning.

DON'T BUILD SUSPENSE WITH THE HOLY SPIRIT AND CLOSE IT WITH A CHECKOUT CART.

And if you're truly carrying a word from the Lord, be careful not to commodify it. Because the moment the Word becomes a sales funnel, you're not discipling people, you're enrolling them. And that's not what you were called to do.

Let ministry be ministry. Let business be business. Let the lines be clear. Let the conscience stay clean.

Because righteousness doesn't manipulate. And revival isn't built on upsells.

GOD TOLD ME TO ISN'T A BUSINESS PLAN

Oh, have I ever seen this one play out, so many times. But let me talk about me. There's a danger in the phrase "God told me to." And I'm not talking about when God truly speaks. I'm talking about when we're so committed to our emotions, our will, and our desires that we start to see God who isn't there. We stop discerning and start projecting. And before we know it, we're following the voice of our ambition or emotion instead of the voice of the Holy Spirit.

One of the clearest examples of this in my life was actually pretty recent.

God had been speaking to me, deeply, about feeding His people. I knew that was a word from Him. I knew He wanted me to pour into a few people more intentionally. Discipleship. Personal. Intimate. That part was clear. And I've always had this deep desire to help people grow in the Word, mature in their calling, and know God for themselves. That's who I am.

But here's where it went sideways.

The excitement of the people around me started to become louder than my own discernment. They loved the vision. They hyped me up. They encouraged the "next step" like it was obvious: Platform it. Build a system. Launch the thing. Go big.

So I did. I spent thousands, and I mean thousands, of dollars building platforms, tools, back-ends, automations, you name it. It looked amazing. It made sense. It even started bearing fruit.

BUT UNDER THE SURFACE, RESENTMENT STARTED TO RISE.

I was exhausted. Bitter. Discouraged. And it wasn't because I didn't love the people. It was because the people I was pouring into weren't taking it seriously. They hadn't had a real encounter with God yet, so they treated this holy thing casually, like a side hobby or a convenience. And when your soul is out of alignment, that kind of response can devastate you.

That's when I realized: I had stepped outside of what God told me to do.

He told me to feed His people, not platform it for the masses.

That extra step didn't come from Him. It came from the people. The expectations. The pressure to scale. And because I love deeply and carry weight in the Spirit, I let that love get ahead of the instruction.

I didn't do it out of rebellion. I did it out of passion.

BUT EVEN GOOD INTENTIONS CAN LEAD TO DISOBEDIENCE WHEN WE'RE MORE MOVED BY OUTCOMES THAN OBEDIENCE.

Yes, it bore fruit. But fruit can be deceptive. Just because something is bearing fruit doesn't mean it's the kind of fruit God asked you to grow. And when I finally pulled the plug on it, when I shut down the platform and walked away, some of the people who were benefiting from that system didn't say anything out loud, but their silence said it all. Their shift in posture said it all.

And in that moment, I understood Moses in a way I never had before.

I used to judge him. Like, He told you to speak to the rock, not strike it. Why did you mess that up?

But I found myself there, frustrated, tired, grieving, feeling like I was about to strike something out of pain. And it hit me: I was building something I thought God told me to do, but I had been moved by emotion, excitement, and the voices around me, not the still, quiet voice of the Lord.

This isn't to shame myself. It's to be honest. Because that's how subtle it can be.

If you're not careful, you will start making business decisions and spiritual decisions in God's name that He never co-signed. And when those things crash or drain you dry, you'll be sitting there wondering why it hurts so bad. Why it feels like you're losing your mind. Why the burden feels unbearable. But the truth is: God never asked you to build it like that. The Ishmael was yours. The instruction was different.

So if you find yourself saying, "God told me to", pause. Ask yourself: Am I sure it was Him? Or am I trying to give spiritual language to emotional decisions?

God is not afraid to tell us "no." But if we refuse to hear that "no," we'll always find a way to hear "yes."

And I never want to build like that again.

Dig Deeper

Let's take off the mask and be honest before God. If you're building something in His name, you need to be willing to let Him search your motives, your methods, and your messaging.

Ask yourself:

1. Have I ever used the language of "Kingdom," "God first," or "divine timing" to increase trust, but in reality, I just wanted a sale?

   Do I default to emotional urgency, guilt, or subtle manipulation when people don't respond the way I want them to?

2. Have I spiritualized strategy that was never birthed in prayer, just copied from someone else's funnel?

3. Do I pressure people into support by implying that their loyalty to me reflects their loyalty to God?

4. Have I confused spiritual fruit with financial results?

5. Am I honoring the sacredness of ministry, or blending it into my marketing so seamlessly that people

can't tell where one ends and the other begins?

6. Do I leave people more free, or more dependent, after they work with me?

Take these questions to the secret place. Journal them. Pray through them. Don't rush. Don't defend. Let the Holy Spirit show you the truth. And if something needs to be repented of, do it boldly.

Because manipulation wrapped in scripture is still manipulation.

And your anointing is too precious to be prostituted for performance.

CLEAN HANDS, CLEAR CONSCIENCE

Father,

We come before You, not with pretense or polish, but with open hands and exposed hearts. We confess that in our pursuit of success, we've sometimes blurred the lines. We've used holy language to push worldly agendas. We've let marketing become a mask for manipulation. We've used "God told me" when it was really just "I wanted to."

Forgive us, Lord. Not just for the methods, but for the motives. Not just for the copy, but for the compromise.

We don't want to build platforms You never asked for. We don't want to speak on stages You never sent us to. We don't want to sell from places in our soul that are still striving for validation.

Clean our hands. Purify our hearts. Strip away anything we've built on performance, pressure, or pride. We don't want to lead people through the funnel of our ambition, we want to shepherd them in alignment with Your heart.

Teach us how to separate the sacred from the strategic. Teach us how to steward both calling and commerce with clarity and conviction. Remind us that ministry is not a lead magnet, and the anointing is not a marketing tool.

God, we want clean business. Clean hearts. Clean conscience.

May our words reflect Your truth. May our actions reveal Your character. May our strategies be pure enough to lay at Your feet without shame.

Let our lives, our businesses, our messages, our ministries, testify that righteousness is not our branding. It's our posture before You.

We don't want influence without integrity. We don't want impact without intimacy. We want to build what You can bless.

And when the temptation comes to manipulate, monetize, or manufacture momentum in Your name, arrest us, Lord. Shut it down. Remind us that favor doesn't come from funnels. It comes from walking uprightly before You.

We yield every tactic. Every tool. Every launch. Every offer. Every word.

Because You are the strategy.

In Jesus' name,

Amen.

Righteousness in the Marketplace

CHAPTER 6

RIGHTEOUSNESS PROTECTS THE SACRED

WHAT IT MEANS TO PROTECT THE SACRED

When Scripture speaks of what is sacred, it doesn't use the English word sacred in the King James Version. But the concept runs through every page of the Word. The first time it appears is in Genesis 2:3, where God "blessed the seventh day, and sanctified it." The Hebrew word there is qadash (Strong's H6942), meaning to consecrate, to set apart, to make holy, to treat as not common.

That's what sacred is: something God Himself declares untouchable, set apart, reserved for His glory. It is not casual. It is not common. Webster's 1828 defines it as "consecrated, or set apart, dedicated to a holy use; not profane or common; entitled to reverence." And that is exactly what rises in the spirit when we hear sacred: it's what God holds dear.

For the believer, this reality touches everything. The moment we committed our lives to Christ, we became vessels of consecration. Our families, our friendships, our marriages, our money, our work, our businesses, all of it is qadash.

Not because of the label we put on it, but because of the covenant we entered into with God. To profane what He calls sacred is not just bad strategy, it's sin.

This is where the line gets blurred in our generation. Too many treat business as if it has nothing to do with God, as if entrepreneurship exists in a "neutral" category. But there is no neutral ground in the Kingdom. What we build, the way we lead, the motives that drive us, all of it is either consecrated or corrupted. There is no middle.

Think about Jesus. Think about Paul. Both men lived boldly, with great influence, and at times they had more than enough. Yet they also knew how to work with their hands, how to suffer lack without cutting corners, and how to pay the price for the sake of obedience. They never blurred the line between what was sacred and what was common. They understood that the Kingdom is not measured in optics or outcomes, it is measured in faithfulness. Jesus Himself prayed for us in John 17:15:

> *"I'M NOT ASKING YOU TO TAKE THEM OUT OF THE WORLD, BUT TO KEEP THEM SAFE FROM THE EVIL ONE" (NLT).*

That phrase evil one is translated from the Greek word ponēros, which carries a deeper meaning than just "Satan." It points to toil, oppression, moral harm, and corruption. Jesus wasn't only praying for us to be spared from the devil's attacks, He was asking the Father to deliver us from systems of toil, from dehumanizing work, from burnout, from corruption and compromise that strip the soul.

This is the difference between a toil mindset and a kingdom mindset of rest:

> **Toil mindset:** rooted in fear of lack, obsessed with achievement, anxious about legacy, filling every moment with busyness and distraction, building identity on productivity, measuring worth by possessions, exploiting people to get ahead.
>
> **Kingdom rest:** rooted in obedience, established in rhythms of worship and Sabbath, confident in God's provision, holding resources with an open hand, storing treasures in heaven, building legacy through eternal fruit (John 15:16), and loving people freely without making them transactions.

Toil is the mindset of Egypt. Rest is the mindset of the Kingdom. One enslaves you to production; the other frees you to steward. One measures your worth by what you do; the other anchors your worth in who you belong to.

THAT'S WHY BUSINESS CAN NEVER BE NEUTRAL FOR THE BELIEVER. TO RUN A BUSINESS WITHOUT CONSECRATION IS TO BLUR THE LINE BETWEEN SACRED AND COMMON.

To cut corners, to exploit, to manipulate, to chase desires without delighting in the Lord, that is to build Babel all over again. But to honor God in every decision, every client interaction, every system, every sale, that is to build something qadash. That is to protect what is sacred.

WHY WE BLUR SACRED BOUNDARIES

If the previous section laid the foundation that everything is qadash, set apart, consecrated to God, then we must ask the hard question: why do so many blur the line between sacred and common? Why do leaders take what is meant to be holy and treat it as if it is theirs to exploit?

The answer isn't just surface-level insecurity. It goes deeper, into a system of toil that has been running since Babylon. In Scripture, Babylon wasn't just a place, it was a mindset, an economy, a spiritual system. Nebuchadnezzar built a kingdom where wealth came from exploitation, trading, and gaining at the expense of others. This is the same spirit Isaiah condemned when he spoke of Tyre:

> *"AND IT SHALL COME TO PASS AFTER THE END OF SEVENTY YEARS, THAT THE LORD WILL VISIT TYRE, AND SHE SHALL TURN TO HER HIRE, AND SHALL COMMIT FORNICATION WITH ALL THE KINGDOMS OF THE WORLD UPON THE FACE OF THE EARTH. AND HER MERCHANDISE AND HER HIRE SHALL BE HOLINESS TO THE LORD..." (ISAIAH 23:17–18, KJV)*

Tyre prostituted her glory, selling integrity for profit. That's the picture of what happens any time economic exploitation becomes idolatry. It is spiritual adultery.

And the same spirit is alive today. Look around and you'll see Babylon's fingerprints everywhere:

- Sweatshops where human beings are treated like disposable machines.

- Unfair wages with no benefits, where workers are barely surviving while corporations thrive.

- Industries built on addiction, pornography, gambling, predatory lending.

- Human trafficking, where lives are sold and traded like currency.

But it doesn't stop at the global level. It seeps into relationships. Parents treating children transactionally, love withheld unless achievement meets a certain standard. Friendships maintained for influence or connections rather than joy or covenant. Even sexuality and charm turned into currency to buy access, power, or attention.

And perhaps most dangerous: it seeps into the church. Ministries begin to operate more like businesses, treating the gospel as a product and faith as a brand. Sermons are shaped to please donors instead of God. Leaders sell spiritual access, charging for prophetic words, manipulating fundraising, promising miracles in exchange for money. They trade the sacred for sales and call it strategy.

You know the fruit when you see it. Identity becomes tied to sales, likes, and followers instead of obedience. Hard truths are avoided to keep clients or crowds happy. Manipulation takes root, promising blessings or breakthrough if people will just buy the product or sow the seed. God-talk becomes the sales hook, not the conviction of the heart.

This is the psychology of exploitation. At its root, it is a trauma response. When someone grows up in environments where worth is tied to performance, love is tied to achievement, or survival depends on staying visible, they carry those wounds into business. Oversharing becomes a way to secure validation. Exploiting others becomes a way to stay safe, relevant, or resourced.

THE HUSTLE FEELS HOLY BECAUSE IT FEEDS THE CRAVING FOR APPROVAL, BUT IT'S STILL BONDAGE. IT'S STILL TOIL.

And toil is exactly what Jesus prayed we would be delivered from. When He asked the Father in John 17 to "keep them from the evil one," the Greek word used is ponēros. It doesn't just mean Satan, it also means toil, corruption, and oppression. In other words, Jesus prayed that His people would be kept from the very system that exhausts, manipulates, and destroys the sacred.

Here's the truth: you cannot heal a toil mindset with more toil. You cannot silence insecurity with more visibility. And you cannot prove worth by exploiting what God called sacred.

That's why my coaching practice is built differently. Yes, I'm prophetic. Yes, I am a woman of God. But I refuse to sell prophecy or spiritual access. I'm also a certified life coach and a lifelong student of psychology, actively pursuing higher education in the field. That means when you coach with me, you're not buying a shortcut, you're committing to the hard work of transformation.

We set goals. We confront limiting beliefs. We dig into Scripture, but we also examine where those patterns came from psychologically. We build emotional intelligence, practice regulating emotions, and expose "stinking thinking" for what it is, the enemy's attacks on the mind. We use tools to renew thought patterns and map new neurological pathways. And yes, when I can, I connect clients to resources in my network, web developers, marketers, strategists, investors, but I never promise overnight riches. Why? Because I don't hold that power.

> DEUTERONOMY 8:18 SAYS IT CLEARLY: "REMEMBER THE LORD YOUR GOD. HE IS THE ONE WHO GIVES YOU POWER TO BE SUCCESSFUL..." (NLT).

I can equip. I can teach. I can walk with you. But only God gives wealth. Only God opens the floodgates. My role is to help you shut the doors the enemy has used, grow in wisdom, and build on a foundation that God Himself can bless.

That's the difference between Babylon's system and the Kingdom of God. Babylon manipulates. The Kingdom equips.

BABYLON SELLS ACCESS. THE KINGDOM OFFERS COVENANT.

Babylon treats people as transactions. The Kingdom treats people as treasures.

So if you find yourself tempted to exploit someone's words, moments, or vulnerability for reach or revenue, pause. Ask yourself: is this Babylon or is this Kingdom? Is this toil or is this rest? Is this manipulation or is this ministry?

Because at the end of the day, blurred sacred boundaries don't just cost you credibility, they cost you consecration. And when consecration is lost, blessing cannot remain.

And exploitation does not always look like sweatshops or corporate greed. Sometimes it looks as simple as how we handle someone's trust in the age of social media.

REVERENCE OVER REACH

Not everything needs to be screenshotted and shared.

We've crossed a line in this culture, one that most people haven't even stopped to notice.

We've started turning private moments of vulnerability, gratitude, and trust into public content.

And it's dishonorable.

Someone sends you a heartfelt message, thanking you for how your words or work impacted them.

They didn't comment publicly.

They didn't tag you.

They came to you privately.

That wasn't just feedback.

That was a moment.

A moment where they felt safe. Seen.

Where they took down their guard and chose to share something human with you. And instead of honoring that sacred exchange, we screenshot it and toss it on a feed like a trophy.

"Look at what someone said about me. Look at how good my program is. Look at this proof."

No.

That wasn't yours to post.

They came to you, not your audience.

They opened up in private for a reason.

Even if the words are positive, even if they're uplifting, that does not mean it's yours to exploit.

It means they trusted you.

And instead of nurturing that trust, we're prostituting it for praise, reach, and engagement.

We've become so addicted to visibility and validation that we don't even realize we're breaking something holy.

Something human.

And let's be clear, this isn't exposure.

This isn't calling out abuse.

This isn't justice.

This is marketing.

This is turning human moments into ad copy.

And it needs to stop.

Because when someone tells you, "Thank you. That helped me," your first instinct shouldn't be, "Let me post this."

It should be, "Let me honor this."

TURNING REVERENCE INTO REVENUE: THE REAL COST OF EXPLOITING INTIMACY

Let's call it what it really is.

You sensed the weight of that message the moment it hit your inbox. It wasn't a casual comment, it was a sacred trust.

You didn't share that testimony to glorify God, you shared it to validate your offer.

You didn't post that message because it blessed you, you posted it because it would boost engagement.

And somewhere deep down, you knew it.

We've sanitized spiritual manipulation by rebranding it as influence.

But influence without restraint is just ego with good lighting.

You're not sharing a win, you're monetizing trust.

You're not edifying the body, you're

editing people's vulnerability into marketing material.

You're not leading, you're leveraging. If you're using people's private words as public proof without their full-hearted, eyes-open consent,

you're not walking in integrity.

You're functioning like Balaam, someone who once heard from God, but sold that voice for proximity to power.

When praise turns into currency, and encouragement becomes a launch strategy, we've stopped being ministers and started becoming merchants of sacred things.

WHAT THE BIBLE SAYS ABOUT REVERENCE AND RESTRAINT

We don't need to guess how God feels about those who parade their good deeds for attention.

> "WATCH OUT! DON'T DO YOUR GOOD DEEDS PUBLICLY, TO BE ADMIRED BY OTHERS, FOR YOU WILL LOSE THE REWARD FROM YOUR FATHER IN HEAVEN." – MATTHEW 6:1 (NLT)

This isn't just about money or service. It's about motive.

When the goal is admiration, we've already lost the reward.

When our instinct is to harvest content instead of protect confidence, we're no longer stewards, we're spectators playing for applause.

> *"A GOSSIP GOES AROUND TELLING SECRETS, BUT THOSE WHO ARE TRUSTWORTHY CAN KEEP A CONFIDENCE." – PROVERBS 11:13 (NLT)*

> *"A TIME TO TEAR AND A TIME TO MEND. A TIME TO BE QUIET AND A TIME TO SPEAK." – ECCLESIASTES 3:7 (NLT)*

Not everything is meant to be said. Not everything is meant to be shown. Wisdom discerns the difference.

THE PSYCHOLOGY BEHIND THE POST

There's a deep human craving for validation. Social media feeds that desire like a drug. Every share, like, and comment tells us: You matter. You're seen. You're successful.

But when we turn private affirmations into public proof, we reinforce a dangerous message:

That something only matters if others see it.

This breaks down the integrity of trust. It teaches us to value optics over intimacy. And it rewires our leadership identity to become dependent on constant external affirmation.

That's not spiritual maturity. That's emotional codependency wrapped in branding language.

STRATEGIC WISDOM: WHEN AND HOW TO SHARE

There's nothing wrong with testimonials.
There's nothing wrong with gratitude.

But there's everything wrong with co-opting a private moment without consent. If someone sends you a message and you think it could help others:

1. Ask permission. Not just a checkbox consent, ask if they're truly comfortable having their words shared.
2. Honor context. If it was said in confidence, it was meant to stay in confidence.
3. Discern the motive. Are you posting to help someone else, or just to boost your image?
4. Check your own heart. Are you still satisfied even if the story never goes public?

Because sacred things don't need a platform to be powerful.

They need to be protected.

LET'S REBUILD HONOR IN THE WAY WE LEAD

Some moments need to be sheltered.

Some stories need to be stewarded, not shared.

Some thank-yous are not testimonials.

They're sacred echoes of what God is doing behind the scenes.

And if we can't tell the difference,

we're not building a platform.

We're building a machine that eats people alive.

Let your reverence outweigh your reach.

Let your integrity outshine your insights.

Let your private altar matter more than your public algorithm.

Because when someone entrusts you with a moment, heaven is watching to see what you'll do with it.

And not everything that touches your inbox belongs on your feed.

YOU'RE NOT BUILDING A PLATFORM. YOU'RE BUILDING A PEOPLE.

Yes, marketing matters.

Yes, communication matters.

If you're building a business, it's wise to learn strategy, messaging, and structure.

God is a God of order, and there's nothing wrong with using skill to serve well.

But at what cost?

Because somewhere along the way, many people, especially people of faith, have stopped building platforms that heal and help… and started building machines that eat people alive.

Righteousness in the Marketplace

WE'VE TRADED SOUL FOR SCALE. DISCERNMENT FOR DATA. INTIMACY FOR INFLUENCE.

And the scariest part?

It's all in the name of "growth."

We don't even stop to ask:

- Is this still serving, or just converting?
- Is this still loving, or just automated?
- Is this actually helping people heal and thrive, or just pushing products and praise reports to stay visible?

We throw someone's vulnerable inbox message on a public feed without a second thought.

We turn thank-you notes into testimonials before we even ask permission.

We chase high-ticket and high-visibility opportunities and call it "impact,"

but the people on the other side are often

exhausted, disillusioned, and poorer in every sense of the word.

And that's not ministry.

That's not excellence.

That's extraction.

Let's be clear: this is no longer about stewarding what God gave you.

It's about monetizing what people give you, and calling it stewardship.

This isn't about whether your business is labeled "Christian" or not.

Most of the people you'll serve may never set foot in a church, and they shouldn't have to.

Because your character is the sermon.

- The way you respond to emails.
- The way you honor someone's story.
- The way you refund with dignity, deliver with excellence, and treat people when no one's watching.

That's what reveals who reigns in your heart.

There's a difference between using systems and letting systems use you.

There's a difference between automated delivery and automatic disconnection.

There's a difference between scale and soul.

Too many entrepreneurs have lost sight of what they set out to do because the metrics became more important than the mission. You can't measure spiritual fruit in click-through rates. And you can't disciple a generation if all they ever get from you is a pre-scheduled funnel.

So yes, build the business.

Learn the systems.

Structure well.

But filter every tactic through the Spirit.

Righteousness in the Marketplace

Because if the only way your platform works is by using people...

If the only way you stay credible is by constantly proving who likes you...

If the only way you feel valuable is by posting someone else's praise...

You may not be building what you think you're building.

You're not called to run a machine.

You're called to lead with mercy, wisdom, and clarity.

You're not called to sell your impact.

You're called to embody it.

And if God is truly at the center of what you're building,

then people, all people, should feel more whole after encountering it.

Not more used.

Let's build with integrity.

Let's communicate with reverence.

Let's do business in a way that tells the truth about who we belong to.

Because the real fruit of your work will never be your revenue.

It'll be the residue you leave behind, in the hearts, minds, and spirits of those who trusted you enough to let you in.

Dig Deeper

1. Where in my life or business have I treated something consecrated (qadash) as common?
2. Have I blurred sacred boundaries by using people's trust, stories, or words for my own validation or visibility?
3. Am I building from Kingdom rest, or am I caught in Babylon's cycle of toil, exploitation, and transaction?

4. In what ways have I been tempted to measure my worth by sales, likes, or applause instead of obedience to God?
5. If God asked me to keep a win private, unseen by the crowd, would I still see it as valuable, or would I feel like it "doesn't count" unless it's public?

CONSECRATE IT AGAIN

The call is simple but costly: consecrate it again.

Your business. Your influence. Your voice. Your relationships. Your money. Every part of your life that God entrusted to you, it is not common. It is not yours to exploit. It is qadash, set apart.

Heaven is watching not just what you build but how you build it. And integrity is not proven in what you post, but in what you protect. The inbox moment you keep private, the story you refuse to leverage, the client you honor when no one is watching, these are the altars where God sees and rewards.

The world may measure success by reach and revenue, but the Kingdom measures it by reverence. You are not called to run a machine, you are called to steward a people. You are not called to trade in sacred things, you are called to embody them.

So let this be your prayer as you close this chapter:

"Lord, I consecrate it all again. Protect my heart from the spirit of toil. Guard my motives from Babylon's system. Teach me to honor what is sacred. And let the way I build reflect the One I belong to."

Righteousness in the Marketplace

The blessing is not in the applause of men but in the approval of heaven. Build with that in mind. Build with that in heart. And when the temptation comes to trade reverence for reach, may you remember, you are not a merchant of sacred things. You are a steward of holy ones.

PART III - CONSTRUCTING WITH HEAVEN'S PATTERN

Righteousness in the Marketplace

CHAPTER 7

WHOLENESS MAKES YOU WISE

WHOLENESS IS NOT PERFECTION, IT'S YIELDING

Wholeness is not the absence of weakness. It is the presence of wisdom. It is knowing when to pause, when to seek counsel, when to heal, and when to let the Holy Spirit finish what your own strength cannot.

A whole person isn't flawless, they are aware. They know where they end and where God begins. They recognize the difference between emotion and discernment, between reaction and response. They understand that the goal of spiritual maturity isn't control, it's surrender.

Too often, we mistake wholeness for perfection. We think it means never struggling, never failing, never needing help. But the Word teaches something far richer. Wholeness in Christ is not achieved; it is received. It is the continual process of letting the Spirit sanctify every fractured place until what flows from you reflects the One who dwells in you.

Think of David. Passionate. Impulsive. Deeply human. He was driven by what he felt, and many times it cost him. But when conviction hit, David didn't hide. He poured himself out before God. The Psalms are proof, his personal journal of repentance, worship, anguish, and longing. He was not perfect, but he was honest. And honesty is what allowed healing to happen. That humility is what made him whole.

Think of Solomon. The man who once carried divine wisdom and later drowned in indulgence. For years he built, collected, and pursued everything under the sun, and discovered it was all vanity. Yet, even in his disillusionment, we find redemption. Ecclesiastes isn't the journal of a man who lost wisdom; it's the confession of a man who learned the cost of living without it. When Solomon returned to God, he realized that wisdom apart from obedience only leads to emptiness. That return, that repentance, was wholeness being restored.

Think of Paul. The thorn in his flesh wasn't punishment, it was preservation. When he begged God to take it away, God replied,

> *"MY GRACE IS SUFFICIENT FOR YOU, FOR MY POWER WORKS BEST IN WEAKNESS" (2 CORINTHIANS 12:9, NLT).*

Grace is God's divine enablement, His power at work in your limitation. Wholeness, then, isn't the removal of struggle but the revelation of grace within it. Paul learned that dependence is strength, not deficiency.

And finally, think of Jesus. The Son of God who withdrew to pray when pressure mounted. In Gethsemane, He didn't strategize an escape plan, He surrendered. He said,

> *"FATHER, IF YOU ARE WILLING, REMOVE THIS CUP FROM ME; NEVERTHELESS NOT MY WILL, BUT YOURS BE DONE." (LUKE 22:42, ESV).*

That prayer was not weakness, it was wisdom. It was the wholeness of perfect obedience.

All four stories echo the same truth:

WHOLENESS IS WHAT ALLOWS US TO LEAD WITHOUT WOUNDING OTHERS.

It produces wisdom because it teaches us to lead from healed places instead of hidden pain.

When you're whole, you don't project your unhealed places onto people. You don't build out of insecurity. You don't strive for validation or control outcomes to feel safe. You become a vessel that God can trust, one who leads, corrects, and creates from purity rather than pain.

Wholeness makes you wise because it teaches you how to stay human and holy at the same time, fully aware of your limits, yet fully reliant on God's limitless grace.

DISCERNMENT COMES FROM WHOLENESS

Wholeness brings clarity. When you are healed, you stop chasing labels and start honoring function. You no longer need titles to validate your identity, you need discernment to protect what is holy. That's why maturity matters so much right now: not every trailblazer is an apostle.

There's a growing trend in Christian entrepreneurial spaces where being visionary, prolific, or bold is often equated with being apostolic. If you've started multiple businesses, led a few churches, or launched a personal brand that impacts others, someone has probably told you that you "carry an apostolic mantle." But when sacred language gets diluted, so does sacred function. The word apostle was never meant for marketing. It isn't a synonym for leadership capacity or innovation, it's a spiritual office with a holy assignment. And if we don't protect the meaning of this word, we'll keep confusing charisma with calling and followers with fruit.

APOSTLESHIP IS NOT A FLEX

The word apostle comes from the Greek apostolos, "one who is sent." It's a compound word: apo (from) and stellō (to send). Apostles were commissioned envoys who carried the full authority of the One who sent them. They didn't speak for themselves. They carried the message, heart, and culture of their Sender.

In Hebrew culture, the same idea was expressed through the word shaliach, a legal representative sent to act on another's behalf. To reject the shaliach was to reject the one who sent him. The role wasn't symbolic; it was binding.

When Jesus chose the Twelve and later appeared to Paul, He wasn't gathering fans. He was commissioning representatives, men who would carry His message into spiritually barren places and establish Kingdom order. Apostleship wasn't about visibility; it was about responsibility.

BEFORE YOU EVER DESIRE THE TITLE, ASK YOURSELF: ARE YOU READY FOR THE WEIGHT? ARE YOU PREPARED TO BE MISUNDERSTOOD, REJECTED, OR EVEN STRIPPED OF INFLUENCE FOR THE SAKE OF OBEDIENCE?

Apostleship is not a brand upgrade; it's a cross to carry. They don't just launch, they anchor. They don't just inspire, they correct. They don't just build, they confront disorder, bring alignment, and carry the burden of spiritual responsibility whether people applaud or not.

So no, starting multiple ventures doesn't automatically make someone apostolic. Visibility is not authority. Productivity is not proof. Wholeness teaches you that. When your heart is healed, you no longer need big titles to feel significant, you need integrity to stay aligned.

WHY THIS MISUSE MATTERS

When we label every high-capacity leader an apostle, we flatten the depth of what apostleship really is. We cheapen what Paul endured and what Christ commissioned. We exchange accountability for aesthetics. Entrepreneurs are often visionary, strategic, and driven, but those traits alone don't define apostleship. You can be a groundbreaker and not be a sent one. You can build big and still lack Kingdom culture. Apostleship isn't about going first; it's about going on behalf.

That distinction requires wisdom, and wisdom flows from wholeness. Only a healed leader can discern the difference between divine sending and self-promotion. Only a whole heart can carry authority without needing attention.

PAUL WASN'T BUILDING A BRAND

When you read Paul's letters, you don't meet a man obsessed with optics. You meet a man obsessed with truth.

He didn't write to boost engagement; he wrote to bring correction and strengthen faith. His apostleship wasn't proven by numbers but by endurance, tested in prisons, confirmed in scars, and sealed by obedience.

That's why his clarity still pierces centuries later. Because in a world that equates exposure with credibility, Paul reminds us that spiritual weight comes from obedience in obscurity.

If Paul lived today, he'd still be writing long-form truth, not for applause, but for alignment. Not to go viral, but to bear fruit that remains.

THE REAL APOSTOLIC MEASURE

Let's be clear:
- Apostles don't just build, they bring order.
- Apostles don't just lead, they carry.
- Apostles don't just teach, they go where others won't and establish what others fear to confront.

This doesn't make them superior, it makes them responsible. True apostleship carries the burden of clarity, the sting of correction, and the willingness to walk alone when necessary. It's not a vibe; it's a vow.

So let's stop handing out apostolic titles like personality types. Let's return to the Word, to function, to fruit. Because not every trailblazer is an apostle, not every builder is sent, and not every loud voice is a Kingdom one.

But if you are sent, and you know it, walk in it.

Not with swagger, but with sobriety.

Not with hype, but with holiness.

Because wholeness will teach you that obedience is enough, and the fruit will follow.

THE PSYCHOLOGY OF WHOLENESS AND WISDOM

Wisdom doesn't only come from knowing the Word, it comes from being healed enough to apply it.

A wounded mind can memorize Scripture and still misinterpret it through pain. A healed mind can hear the same verse and recognize both instruction and invitation. That's why inner healing and emotional intelligence are not optional for Kingdom leaders, they are prerequisites for discernment.

When we're unhealed, our leadership becomes reactionary.

We make quick decisions because stillness feels unsafe.

We overexplain because rejection feels fatal.

We micromanage because control feels like protection.

And we call it excellence, when it's really anxiety in disguise.

But when we're whole, the noise settles. We begin to pause before responding. We stop needing to prove our point or push our way. Wholeness allows space between trigger and truth, and that space is where wisdom lives.

HOW UNHEALED LEADERS THINK

Unhealed leaders often confuse urgency with importance.

They measure value by visibility and believe stillness equals laziness. Their nervous system stays locked in overdrive, constantly scanning for threat or failure. That hypervigilance masquerades as ambition.

Trauma, whether from betrayal, scarcity, or early survival, teaches the brain that safety comes through performance. The same drive that once kept you alive can later keep you from peace. That's why many high-capacity believers mistake adrenaline for anointing. They confuse stress hormones for spiritual stamina. But wisdom doesn't flow in fight-or-flight. It flows in rest.

It's birthed in regulated minds and submitted hearts.

THE WHOLENESS CYCLE

Wholeness doesn't mean you never get triggered. It means you know how to handle the trigger without letting it handle you.

Here's the cycle:

1. **Awareness** – You recognize what's rising in you instead of projecting it on others.
2. **Honesty** – You name the emotion before the Lord instead of numbing it.

3. **Surrender** – You invite the Holy Spirit to speak truth to the wound.
4. **Integration** – You practice new habits that align with healing rather than fear.

Repeat this long enough and wisdom becomes reflexive. You start hearing the Spirit in real time because the clutter inside of you is finally quiet enough for His voice to register.

EMOTIONALLY INTELLIGENT LEADERSHIP

Emotionally intelligent leaders don't suppress emotion, they steward it. They can tell the difference between righteous anger and reactive anger, between divine urgency and panic. They listen deeply before they lead boldly.

That's what makes their wisdom trustworthy. Because wholeness teaches empathy. And empathy is one of the most under-preached fruits of the Spirit. When you're whole, you can hold tension without collapsing. You can correct without condemning. You can hear feedback without shame. You can release people without resentment. That's the psychology of wholeness, regulation that reflects redemption.

RENEWING THE MIND, REGULATING THE HEART

Romans 12:2 tells us to be transformed by the renewing of our mind. Neurologically, renewal happens through repetition, retraining thought pathways until the brain learns safety in truth. Spiritually, it happens through surrender, allowing God's Word to reshape the way we perceive, process, and perform.

You can't walk in divine wisdom with a dysregulated mind.

 You can't steward people well if their behavior keeps re-wounding your unhealed parts.

 You can't discern spiritual attack from healthy accountability if every correction still sounds like rejection.

This is why the most Spirit-led people are also the most self-aware. They understand that self-awareness isn't self-worship, it's stewardship. The more healed you are, the clearer your hearing becomes.

HEALING BEFORE STRATEGY

Before you design another system or launch another program, ask:

Am I building this from a healed place or a hurried place?

Is this structure emerging from revelation or reaction?

Because what you build emotionally will leak spiritually.

Unhealed ambition will always attract exhausted people.

But healed leadership creates safe ecosystems where others can grow without fear.

Wholeness is not about perfection; it's about partnership, between your healed humanity and God's divine wisdom.

It's the quiet confidence of knowing that your peace is protection, your discernment is direction, and your rest is resistance against the spirit of toil.

And that's what makes you wise.

LEADERSHIP THAT HEALS INSTEAD OF HURTS

Wholeness isn't just about your personal peace, it's about the safety you create for others.

When a leader is fragmented, everyone under their influence feels it. The team becomes tense, the culture becomes cautious, and the mission becomes reactive instead of restorative. But when a leader is whole, people exhale around them. They no longer have to guess which version of you they'll meet today, the anxious one, the defensive one, or the angry one. Wholeness makes you consistent. It makes you safe.

The most dangerous wounds in leadership are often invisible. They hide behind the language of "excellence," "boundaries," or "strategy," but underneath, there's usually fear, fear of being taken advantage of, fear of being forgotten, fear of losing control.

Fear turns leaders into managers of outcomes instead of shepherds of people. But healed leaders know the difference between guarding the vision and grasping for control.

When you're whole, you don't need to be right to stay secure. You don't need to prove yourself to stay relevant. You don't need to keep everyone close to feel loved. You can release people without resentment and correct them without crushing them. Because leadership that flows from healing always produces life.

How Wholeness Changes the Way You Lead

1. **You stop leading for validation and start leading from conviction.** You're no longer chasing applause or fearing rejection. You're simply being faithful to the assignment.
2. **You create culture instead of chaos.** Wholeness allows you to build systems that serve people instead of using people to serve systems.
3. **You handle feedback with maturity.** You no longer interpret correction as rejection. You separate accountability from accusation.

4. **You disciple, not dominate.**

    You don't use your influence to control behavior, you use it to cultivate transformation.

5. **You model humility.**

    You don't pretend to have it all together. You let people see the process so they can trust the fruit.

Dig Deeper

Take a moment to ask yourself:

1. Where in my leadership have I been reacting instead of responding?
2. Do people feel safe to tell me the truth, or do they tiptoe around my triggers?
3. Have I confused control with stewardship?
4. How does my emotional health shape the spiritual health of those I lead?

5. What would my leadership look like if I led from a healed place, not a hurried one?

These questions aren't for guilt, they're for grounding. Healing doesn't happen through performance; it happens through permission. Give the Holy Spirit permission to walk through your leadership with you. Let Him show you where fear has been driving and where grace wants to take the wheel.

WISDOM THAT FLOWS FROM WHOLENESS

Father,

Make us whole so that we can be wise.

Make us wise so that we can be safe.

And make us safe so that we can lead

others into wholeness, not wound them in our process.

We don't want to lead from our insecurities anymore. We don't want to build from fear, control, or exhaustion. We want to lead from rest , the kind that comes from being anchored in You.

Teach us to pause before reacting, to listen before speaking, and to heal before leading. Teach us to see correction as kindness, boundaries as stewardship, and grace as strength.

Lord, we repent for the moments we've made people pay the price for wounds they didn't cause.

We repent for the times we've used pressure as proof of anointing or confusion as a substitute for discernment.

And we surrender every unhealed part of

us that still tries to earn what grace already gave.

Heal the places in us that leadership exposed.

Restore the parts of us that calling has cost.

Rebuild the foundations that were shaken by rejection or pride.

And remind us that wisdom is not a reward for perfection , it's the fruit of humility.

From this day forward, may our leadership bring peace, not pressure.

May our words build people, not brands.

May our systems serve souls, not egos.

And may every space we lead in become a reflection of Your heart , stable, safe, and sacred.

We choose wholeness over hustle, maturity over momentum, and grace over grind.

Because wholeness makes us wise.

And wisdom makes us like You.

In Jesus' name,

Amen.

CHAPTER 8

RIGHTEOUSNESS IN THE SUPPLY CHAIN

THE GOD WHO WEIGHS THE SCALES

Righteousness isn't a buzzword, it's a blueprint.

 Long before modern supply chains, global commerce, or corporate ethics policies, God was already talking about integrity in the marketplace. He has always cared about the scales, the systems, and the people behind them. Because to God, righteousness isn't limited to worship. It includes the way we weigh, measure, and treat others.

> "THE LORD DETESTS THE USE OF DISHONEST SCALES,
> BUT HE DELIGHTS IN ACCURATE WEIGHTS."
> , PROVERBS 11:1 (NLT)

That word detests is strong. In Hebrew, it means something morally repulsive, something that stinks before Him. God doesn't use that word for mistakes or misunderstandings. He uses it for deception, specifically, deception that hides behind a false sense of fairness. When business practices look ethical on the outside but exploit people underneath, heaven calls it an abomination.

Because in God's economy, righteousness and justice are not separate ideas. They are twin pillars. The Hebrew word tsedeq (righteousness) is often paired with mishpat (justice). You cannot have one without the other. Tsedeq speaks of alignment with God's moral order, of things being as they should be. Mishpat speaks of setting wrong things right, of intervening when the balance has been violated. Together, they form the spiritual backbone of every covenant God has ever made with His people.

When God established Israel, He didn't just give them worship laws. **He gave them economic laws:**

- Leave the edges of your fields unharvested so the poor can glean (Leviticus 19:9).

- Pay fair wages without delay (Deuteronomy 24:15).
- Do not use differing weights and measures to deceive (Deuteronomy 25:13-16).

Each of these commands carried the same purpose, to make sure that abundance never came through oppression. Because exploitation always reveals a heart that has forgotten who the true Provider is.

> ISAIAH 61:8 NLT SAYS,
> "FOR I, THE LORD, LOVE JUSTICE;
> I HATE ROBBERY AND WRONGDOING.
> I WILL FAITHFULLY REWARD MY PEOPLE FOR THEIR SUFFERING AND MAKE AN EVERLASTING COVENANT WITH THEM."

This is God's supply chain. It's not driven by profit margins, it's driven by purity of motive. His system runs on honor, stewardship, and trust. Every exchange, every product, every partnership is supposed to reflect His nature: generous, just, and holy.

That's why He keeps weighing the scales. Not just the physical ones in ancient markets, but the invisible ones in modern hearts.

He weighs:

- The motives behind every business decision.
- The integrity behind every invoice.
- The humility behind every leadership post.

To Him, righteousness isn't about what we can justify, it's about what He can bless. When your business practices are built on tsedeq and mishpat, you won't have to worry about visibility or validation. Heaven itself will bear witness to your alignment. Because what God finds righteous, He will always resource.

And that's why this matters so much now. We can't claim to build Kingdom businesses while borrowing Babylon's ethics. We can't keep using the world's measures and expect Heaven's reward. God still weighs the scales.

He still listens to the cries of those mistreated by systems we pretend are "standard."

And He still expects His people to build differently.

We've made Jesus so marketable that most believers wouldn't recognize Him if He overturned their business model.

Let's tell the truth. We've built entire industries, Christian ones, on the idea that peace means passivity and that blessing is a byproduct of branding. But Jesus didn't walk into systems and stroke egos. He walked in, looked around, and started flipping what wasn't righteous.

Matthew, Mark, and Luke each record the moment Jesus walked into the temple and saw financial abuse hiding behind religious rituals. The money changers weren't just exchanging coins. They were exploiting people, especially the poor. They sold sacrificial animals at inflated prices to worshipers who had traveled long distances to honor God. The system was rigged. If you were poor, you either overpaid or went without. And if you went without, you walked away ashamed, like your worship wasn't good enough.

Jesus didn't just rebuke that system. He dismantled it in real time.

He flipped their tables. He scattered their profits. He called them thieves. Inside

God's house.

Not behind closed doors. Not in an email. Out loud. In public.

This was not an impulsive outburst. This was holy protest.

A divine demonstration that said, "God is not in this."

It wasn't just about the money. It was about the message that system sent: that access to God could be bought, and only the wealthy could afford it.

Sound familiar?

We may not be selling doves in our digital storefronts, but some of us are still monetizing brokenness. Selling healing in the form of overpriced programs. Preaching about "freedom" while manipulating people with high-pressure launches. Creating emotional urgency to hit income goals, and then spiritualizing the whole thing with a Bible verse and a tithe.

Let's be clear. Jesus was not against commerce. He was against corruption.

He was not against exchanging goods. He was against exploiting the vulnerable.

He wasn't condemning business itself, He was confronting a system that profited off the pain of those it was supposed to serve. And He still is.

IF JESUS WALKED INTO YOUR BUSINESS, WOULD HE BLESS YOUR STRATEGY, OR FLIP YOUR FUNNEL?

This matters because some of us have convinced ourselves that as long as we pray over the plan, God's okay with how we profit. But righteousness is not a prayer over unethical behavior. It's a lifestyle that refuses to build on manipulation, deceit, or greed.

Look at James.

James 5 wasn't written to unbelievers. It was written to the wealthy within the faith community, those who had gained riches while withholding wages. James doesn't say "God will provide for the poor." He says their cries have reached the ears of the Lord. He speaks to the oppressors. "You have fattened yourselves in the day of slaughter." That's not poetic. That's prophetic. He's saying: you've eaten well at the expense of others, and judgment is coming.

And here's what makes that warning so sobering: James doesn't offer them a soft landing. He doesn't say, "Let's talk about grace." He says, "The wages you failed to pay are crying out." God hears the cries of the people your systems have ignored.

This isn't just about what you sell. It's about how you build.

It's about whether your success is clean, or just cleverly cloaked.

Because God doesn't bless exploitation, even if it's dressed up in Scripture.

SOME OF US HAVE LEARNED HOW TO BE SPIRITUAL IN OUR BRANDING BUT MANIPULATIVE IN OUR DELIVERY.

And the problem with that is, it works. It works in the short term. You'll get the sale. You'll get the growth. But what you won't get is peace. What you won't have is holy confidence when God starts inspecting the foundation of what you've built.

Because He will.

If your supply chain, whether literal or spiritual, is built on exploitation, silence, or sleight of hand, it's not aligned. It may still be functioning. But it's not righteous. Righteousness in the supply chain isn't just about paying people fairly or choosing ethical vendors, though that matters. It's about checking your motives, your methods, and your messaging.

It's about being the same person in private strategy sessions that you are in public livestreams.

It's about building with clean hands and a pure heart, not just to protect your brand, but because you fear the Lord.

Because when Jesus walks into your business, He's not looking at your profit margins. He's looking at the people your systems affect.

He's not checking your testimonials. He's

checking your transactions.

He's not impressed by your growth. He's evaluating your guts.

And He's still flipping tables when righteousness is missing.

So ask yourself: would your systems survive the presence of Jesus?

And if not, would you be willing to flip your own tables before He has to?

Righteousness, then, isn't theoretical. It's measurable, visible in how systems treat the people they touch.

And when those systems become corrupt, God doesn't stay silent.

He weighs the scales, exposes the imbalance, and raises up reformers who are willing to confront what everyone else has learned to tolerate.

That's exactly what Jesus did in the temple courts.

EVERY ACT OF EXPLOITATION BEGINS WITH SELF-DECEPTION.

No one wakes up one day and says, "I want to be corrupt." They drift there. One rationalization at a time.

Scripture calls this drift the searing of the conscience (1 Timothy 4:2), when a person becomes desensitized to conviction. Psychology calls it moral disengagement, when people silence their internal compass through subtle cognitive shifts. Both describe the same spiritual disease: a heart that's learned to justify what God condemns.

Let's unpack how that happens.

1. Fear of Scarcity

Scarcity is one of the oldest lies on earth. It started in Eden when the serpent told Eve she was missing something God was withholding. That lie still drives modern economies, and modern entrepreneurs.

Scarcity whispers, "There's not enough to go around. If you don't take it, someone else will."

And once fear enters the decision-making process, ethics become negotiable.

We cut corners, overcharge, underpay, or justify manipulation because fear convinces us that survival depends on compromise.

But in Kingdom economics, provision is never birthed from panic. It's birthed from trust.

When you believe God is your Source, you stop seeing people as competitors and start seeing them as collaborators.

2. The Illusion of Deservedness

Exploitation often hides under entitlement.

"I've worked hard for this."

"I've sacrificed more than they have."

"I deserve to win."

Those statements sound empowering, but they can mutate into justification for using others as means to an end.

Entitlement distorts stewardship into ownership. It convinces us that blessing means permission to dominate.

But Kingdom leadership always remembers: we are stewards, not sovereigns.

Everything entrusted to us, people, money, influence, belongs to God.

The moment we forget that, we begin to treat others' labor, loyalty, or trust as currency we can spend however we please.

3. Cultural Conditioning

We live in a world that normalizes hustle and rewards burnout.

Entire industries glamorize exhaustion as excellence and exploitation as efficiency.

Even in ministry, leaders are praised for building fast, scaling big, and producing constantly, as if outcomes prove anointing.

This conditioning numbs discernment. It teaches us to celebrate visible success and ignore invisible suffering.

But righteousness calls for a different rhythm.

Jesus wasn't in a hurry. He worked from rest, not for rest. His ministry was efficient because His motives were clean. He didn't exploit people to reach goals, He served them to reveal truth.

4. Moral Substitution

This is when people offset compromise in one area by doing good in another.

It sounds like:

"I may not pay fairly, but I tithe."

"I manipulate a little, but it's for the greater good."

"I cut corners, but I give to charity."

That's not integrity, that's accounting.

WE CAN'T BRIBE GOD WITH SELECTIVE OBEDIENCE.

True righteousness isn't about balancing good and bad deeds, it's about surrendering the whole self to truth.

5. Dehumanization

The final step of exploitation is the most dangerous: forgetting that the people affected by our systems have souls.

When profit becomes more important than people, faces turn into metrics, and relationships become transactions.

That's when Babylon's spirit fully takes

over, a system that feeds on the dignity of others to preserve its image of success.

Dehumanization allows exploitation to continue because it numbs empathy.

But wholeness restores empathy.

And empathy is the first sign that righteousness is returning to the heart.

WHY PSYCHOLOGY MATTERS TO THE KINGDOM

Understanding these mental and emotional mechanisms isn't "worldly", it's wise.

It helps us recognize when fear, pride, or self-justification start masquerading as strategy.

It allows us to pause before crossing a line that the Holy Spirit has already illuminated.

And it reminds us that righteousness is not just a moral stance, it's a psychological realignment with truth.

When your business or ministry reflects that inner alignment, you don't just operate ethically, you operate prophetically.

Because every righteous system becomes a prophetic statement to a corrupt world:

"It is possible to prosper without exploitation."

Section 4 – Dig Deeper

Before you move on, take a breath.

This isn't just another chapter to read, it's a mirror to sit with.

The Lord doesn't reveal corruption to condemn us. He reveals it to cleanse us.

He exposes the scales not to shame us but to realign us with His heart.

As you reflect on your business, leadership, or creative work, ask the Holy Spirit to search your motives with precision and mercy. Then, take these questions one at a time. Write. Pray. Don't rush.

1. The Scale of Motives

Have I ever justified an unethical choice because I believed it was "necessary" for success?

What fear or belief was I protecting when I made that decision?

2. The Scale of Stewardship

Am I treating people, clients, employees, or followers, as image-bearers or as resources?

Would I still handle them the same way if no one ever found out how I operate behind closed doors?

3. The Scale of Fairness

Do I pay people what they are worth, or only what I can get away with?

If Jesus examined my invoices, my contracts, or my collaborations, would they reflect justice (mishpat) and righteousness (tsedeq)?

4. The Scale of Transparency

Do my systems, financial, operational, or spiritual, require secrecy to stay profitable?

What would I have to hide if God suddenly flipped my tables?

5. The Scale of Rest

Do I build from Kingdom rest or Babylonian toil?

Have I confused urgency with obedience?

What would it look like to rebuild my rhythms around trust rather than pressure?

6. The Scale of Empathy

When I make business decisions, do I think about the people on the other side of them?

Have I ever numbed myself to the real human cost of convenience, competition, or control?

7. The Scale of Consecration

Is my business truly qadash, set apart, or have I blurred the sacred with the strategic?

If the Lord asked me to rebuild from scratch, what practices or partnerships would I leave behind?

Sit with what the Spirit shows you.

Wholeness begins with awareness.

Righteousness begins with repentance.

And wisdom begins when you let conviction turn into correction.

Because the same God who weighs the scales also restores the balance.

BUILD WHAT HEAVEN CAN BLESS

Father,
 we've read these words, and we feel their weight.
 We've seen the tables You still flip, the scales You still examine,
 and the systems in our own hands that You've been calling to account.
 But today, we choose response over resistance.
 We choose repentance over rationalization.
 We choose righteousness over results.
 Teach us again what it means to build with clean hands.
 To hire with honor.

Righteousness in the Marketplace

To sell with sincerity.

To steward with fear of the Lord, not fear of missing out.

Remind us that the favor we seek cannot be manufactured by marketing,

because Your favor flows where integrity stands.

God, let every contract, collaboration, and conversation in our supply chain pass through Your eyes before it reaches ours.

Strip away anything that exploits, manipulates, or oppresses.

Deliver us from Babylon's methods, its urgency, its vanity, its pride.

Anchor us in Your wisdom so deeply that even when pressure rises, we refuse to compromise the sacred.

And when success comes, because it will, keep us humble enough to remember Who sent it.

May our growth never outpace our gratitude,
our reach never outrun our reverence.
Let righteousness be the unseen thread that runs through every transaction.
Let mercy sit at every table we build.
Let justice echo in every system we design.
And let our businesses become living altars that testify,
that prosperity and purity can coexist.
Because, Lord, we don't want to build what merely works.
We want to build what Heaven can bless.
In Jesus' name,
Amen.

Righteousness in the Marketplace

CHAPTER 9

WISDOM IN THE DIGITAL AGE

IT'S NOT THE TOOL. IT'S THE MINDSET

A meme made its rounds online recently: "Your future doctor is using ChatGPT to pass med school, so now's a good time to start looking after your own health."
It was meant to be funny. But if you pause long enough to look beneath the sarcasm, it's actually revealing.

It reveals a mindset more than a moment. One that doesn't just resist change, it mocks it. It hides behind laughter, but it's built on fear. And worse, it wears the language of wisdom while retreating into suspicion, cynicism, and mental laziness.

THIS ISN'T ABOUT WHETHER YOU USE AI. IT'S ABOUT WHETHER YOU'RE STILL USING YOUR MIND.

Because what I see happening, especially in Christian spaces, isn't a healthy critique of innovation. It's an unhealthy dependence on fear as a default setting. We start labeling every advancement as dangerous without asking deeper questions. We spiritualize our discomfort, slap a verse on our suspicion, and call it discernment when it's really just distrust in disguise.

Let's go there.

DISCERNMENT IS MATURITY. SUSPICION IS FEAR.

The Word is clear:

> "SOLID FOOD IS FOR THOSE WHO ARE MATURE, WHO THROUGH TRAINING HAVE THE SKILL TO RECOGNIZE THE DIFFERENCE BETWEEN RIGHT AND WRONG" (HEBREWS 5:14, NLT).

That's discernment. It's developed, not downloaded. You train for it. You grow into it. It requires proximity to God and a willingness to engage with complexity, not avoid it.

Discernment is the Spirit-led ability to perceive what's true, what's aligned, and what's dangerous, with accuracy, not assumption. It's not based on vibes. It's not driven by gossip. It's informed by truth, Scripture, and a submitted spirit.

Suspicion is something else entirely. Suspicion is fear wearing spiritual language. It doesn't investigate, it assumes. It doesn't seek clarity, it clings to control.

Here's the difference in plain terms: Discernment asks, "What's the truth here, and what is God showing me?" Suspicion decides, "This is wrong, because it makes me uncomfortable or unfamiliar."

Suspicion is reactive. It's defensive. It's rooted in fear of deception, but it often becomes deception itself because it refuses to be corrected, challenged, or taught.

It makes bold claims with no foundation and calls it "revelation."

It labels anything unfamiliar as a threat and calls it "wisdom."

And it thrives in communities where fear has been normalized as holiness.
You cannot steward what you automatically fear. And you cannot influence what you don't understand.

AI ISN'T THE REAL THREAT. COMPLACENCY IS.

Let's say it clearly: ChatGPT isn't the enemy. Technology isn't the problem. Progress is not the antithesis of righteousness. The true threat to the Church, and to your calling, is complacency. It's the willingness to stay stuck in what's familiar because you've mistaken comfort for conviction.
I'm more concerned about the woman who hasn't cracked open a book in five years than I am about the one who's testing AI to

help her brainstorm devotional content. I'm more worried about the Christian entrepreneur who builds everything based on 10-year-old advice than the one who's learning new systems and filtering them through Scripture.

Staying informed isn't carnal. It's responsible.

Being curious isn't worldly. It's wise.

Let's stop pretending that every form of innovation is the enemy's tool. Because if we take that logic to its conclusion, we'd have to reject electricity, modern medicine, the printing press, cars, Wi-Fi, and online banking. We'd all be living off the land in animal skins waiting for God to download handwritten letters from heaven. Most of us aren't about that life. So let's stop pretending like that's the spiritual standard.

CATASTROPHIC THINKING IS NOT A SPIRITUAL GIFT

In psychology, we call it catastrophic thinking, the mental distortion that causes people to expect and prepare for the worst-case scenario in every situation. In spiritual spaces, it sounds like this:

"This is the mark of the beast."

"They're using AI to brainwash people."

"If you're using that platform, you're compromised."

What's really happening? A refusal to do the work of discernment. A lazy adoption of groupthink. A spiritualized paranoia that calls itself prophetic but never points people toward truth, only toward fear, division, and control.

Here's the reality: when the Antichrist system is fully operational, everything will be weaponized. Not just AI. Not just social media. We're talking about food, shelter, banking, communication, and medicine. If the enemy can use it, he will. That's not a surprise. That's Scripture.

But we don't respond to this with fear. We respond with strategy and conviction.

The early Church didn't expand by avoiding the world. They confronted it with truth. They weren't intimidated by Roman systems, they understood how to operate within them while staying loyal to God. They weren't obsessed with identifying the devil in every innovation, they were obsessed with staying filled with the Spirit, studying the Word, and walking in power.

What made them different wasn't how afraid they were of the culture. It was how anchored they were in Christ while living inside of it.

That's what we need now. Not retreats. Not panic. Not spiritual hot takes that sound deep but offer no solution.

GOD ISN'T INTIMIDATED BY AI. HE'S WATCHING WHAT YOU DO WITH IT.

Let's be very clear: God isn't intimidated by artificial intelligence. He's not watching GPT models like some cosmic watchdog hoping to expose their flaws. He's watching us.

Watching how we engage.

Watching how we think.

Watching how we lead others through confusion and complexity.

Watching how we either weaponize fear or disciple people toward wisdom.

This chapter isn't about endorsing tech for tech's sake. It's about calling your mind out of spiritual stagnation. It's about refusing to let fear determine your theology or your decisions.

God is not a God of fear. He is a God of revelation. A God of strategy. A God who gives wisdom without finding fault (James 1:5).

So ask. Seek. Study. Don't outsource your spiritual life to YouTube prophets or your understanding to random group chats. Get in the Word. Learn how systems work. Filter everything through Scripture.

And remember: laziness avoids learning, but wisdom pursues understanding.

That's what spiritual maturity looks like in the digital age.

So no, you don't have to become a tech genius. You don't have to use every new tool. But you do have to steward your mindset. You do have to train your discernment. And you do have to stop spiritualizing small-mindedness as if it's a fruit of the Spirit.

Because the only real threat to your calling isn't AI. It's complacency.

And the only real weapon you need is wisdom.

THE ETHICS OF WISDOM IN A WIRED WORLD

Wisdom is not neutral, it's moral.

And in the digital age, righteousness is revealed not just in what we post, but in how we use power.

Technology, like money, only magnifies what's already in the heart.

If greed is there, innovation becomes

exploitation.

If insecurity is there, visibility becomes idolatry.

If pride is there, platforms become pulpits for self.

But if righteousness is there, the same technology becomes a tool for truth, justice, creativity, and Kingdom advancement.

That's why discernment isn't optional, it's ethical.

Because for believers, the question isn't just "Can I use this?" It's "Should I?"

Should I automate this process if it costs someone else their dignity?

Should I share this content if it damages someone's reputation, even if it gets engagement?

Should I depend on a digital tool for

efficiency if it dulls my dependence on God?

Those aren't tech questions.

They're integrity questions.

One of the most subtle deceptions in our generation is equating convenience with wisdom.

If it's faster, easier, or cheaper, we assume it must be progress.

But sometimes the thing that saves time costs character.

Digital shortcuts are not always spiritual strategies.

Efficiency is not a fruit of the Spirit, self-control is.

And if a tool or trend starts eroding the disciplines that anchor your soul, silence, study, prayer, reflection, it's no longer helping you. It's hollowing you.

This is where many leaders fall.

We get so caught up in managing systems that we stop managing ourselves.

We use analytics as confirmation of anointing.

We measure influence in clicks instead of character.

And before long, we've built something that looks alive online but is dead in the Spirit.

AI CAN'T REPLACE CONVICTION

Let's be honest, artificial intelligence can write a sermon, summarize a study, design a brand, even mimic a voice.

But it cannot bear fruit.

It can reproduce information, not impartation.

It can generate content, not conviction.

And if we start outsourcing our spiritual labor to machines because it's faster, we'll end up with products that sound polished but lack presence.

The danger isn't that AI will replace prophets.

It's that prophets will start acting like algorithms, calculating output instead of cultivating intimacy.

Technology is a gift. But gifts mishandled become idols.

So the call is not to reject innovation but to remain anchored within it, to use wisdom as a firewall around your spirit.

THE DIGITAL LITMUS TEST

Here's a simple way to gauge digital integrity: Would God be pleased with the way I use this tool if no one ever saw the outcome?

If the applause, algorithms, and metrics disappeared, would He still find honor in my process?

Because righteousness isn't about staying relevant.

It's about staying real, before God, before people, and before your own conscience.

Let's stop confusing exposure with effectiveness.

Let's stop chasing visibility when God is asking for virtue.

And let's remember that wisdom, at its core, is not just about what works, it's about what's right.

The digital world doesn't need more Christian influencers.

It needs consecrated thinkers, men and women whose technology use reveals the fear of the Lord, not the fear of irrelevance.

LEARNING TO LEAD ONLINE WITHOUT LOSING YOUR SOUL

If there's one thing this generation has proven, it's that visibility and influence are not the same thing.

You can be seen by thousands and still unseen by Heaven.

You can have reach and no root.

And that's exactly what digital discipleship is meant to confront.

Digital discipleship isn't about getting followers to think like you, it's about helping people think with God.

It's not about curating perfection; it's about cultivating perspective.

It's not about image management; it's about spiritual mentorship.

That means every word you post, every teaching you share, every system you automate is part of someone's formation, whether you realize it or not. You are shaping their worldview, their theology, and even their emotional health.

That's why wisdom online is not optional, it's stewardship.

WHEN CONTENT BECOMES A CALLING

Some people post for attention. Others post for affirmation. But the believer who is called to disciple must post for transformation.

If your content doesn't bring people closer to truth, it's just noise with scripture on it. When Jesus said, "Feed my sheep," He didn't mean "build a brand around your voice." He meant feed them what nourishes, not what flatters.

That means sometimes your online presence will cost you popularity.

It will mean saying the hard thing instead of the trending thing.

It will mean being misjudged, misunderstood, and sometimes mocked for telling the truth.

But that's what leadership in the digital age requires, spiritual stamina to stay faithful when applause is inconsistent and algorithms are unstable.

If you can't be faithful when unseen, you won't be trustworthy when visible.

THE MINISTRY OF SILENCE

The digital age rewards immediacy, but wisdom still speaks slowly.

There is power in being quiet long enough to think, pray, and discern before you post.

Not every revelation is ready for release. Not every insight is meant for the public.

There are times when silence is not avoidance, it's alignment.

Jesus often withdrew to pray.

Moses spent forty days in God's presence before leading Israel.

Even Paul disappeared for three years after his conversion before stepping into ministry.

But we think we need to post every day or risk losing relevance.

Let me tell you something, if silence makes your platform disappear, it was never substance keeping it alive.

Silence sanctifies your motives. It helps you discern what's from the Spirit and what's from your own need to be seen.

LEADERSHIP IN THE AGE OF ALGORITHMS

Algorithms are designed to amplify what gets attention, not what brings transformation.

That means if you let data drive your decisions, you'll eventually dilute your message.

This is where digital discipleship demands courage.

You must decide, Will I feed the algorithm, or feed the people?

Will I shape the content to please crowds, or shape hearts for the Kingdom?

Every time you choose truth over trend, you disrupt the system.

Every time you value obedience over optics, you teach others to do the same. That's what true digital discipleship looks like, it's not about numbers. It's about nurture. It's about equipping a remnant that knows how to think biblically, discern spiritually, and live with integrity no matter how loud the world gets.

YOUR PRESENCE IS THE MESSAGE

You don't have to preach online to disciple people.

The tone of your comments, the humility in your replies, the restraint in your disagreements, these preach louder than your posts ever could.

Every interaction is an opportunity to demonstrate what wholeness looks like in real time.

When people see patience, kindness, and clarity in a digital space filled with chaos, they encounter the Kingdom through you. So whether you're sharing Scripture, running a business, or leading a community online, remember this:

Your presence is your pulpit.

Your posture is your message.

And your peace is your proof.

PROTECTING YOUR MIND IN A CULTURE OF DISTRACTION

If the enemy can't corrupt your morals, he'll distract your mind.

Because distraction is one of the most

sophisticated forms of spiritual warfare in our generation.

You don't have to renounce God to drift from Him, you just have to stay busy.

Busy scrolling.

Busy comparing.

Busy reacting to everyone else's noise until your soul forgets what stillness feels like.

THE CURRENCY OF THE DIGITAL AGE

In ancient times, kingdoms fought over land. In the industrial era, they fought over oil.

In the digital age, the battle is over attention.

Every platform, brand, and algorithm is engineered to capture your gaze, and keep it.

Because wherever your attention goes, your affection follows.

> *THIS IS WHY PROVERBS 4:23 SAYS, "GUARD YOUR HEART ABOVE ALL ELSE, FOR IT DETERMINES THE COURSE OF YOUR LIFE."*

In Hebrew, the word for heart, leb, represents not just emotion, but mind, will, and intellect.

TO GUARD YOUR HEART IS TO GUARD YOUR FOCUS.

And in a world designed to fracture that focus, spiritual warfare now looks like closing tabs, silencing notifications, and giving your full attention back to God.

THE PSYCHOLOGY OF NOISE

Psychologists call it cognitive overload, when constant information prevents the brain from properly processing, storing, and reflecting.

Spiritually, it's what happens when your inner life gets so loud that the still small voice can't break through.

You start mistaking stimulation for revelation.

You confuse momentum with movement.

You begin living reactive instead of responsive, jumping from headline to headline, trend to trend, never noticing that your discernment is growing dull. Every scroll costs you something: presence, awareness, intimacy, peace.

And yet we treat distraction like a harmless habit instead of a spiritual hazard.

THE DISCIPLINE OF FOCUS

Attention is worship.

Whatever you fix your focus on long enough begins to shape your reality.

> *THAT'S WHY ROMANS 12:2 CALLS US TO "BE TRANSFORMED BY THE RENEWING OF YOUR MIND."*

Transformation doesn't happen by inspiration alone, it happens through sustained focus on truth.

You can't renew a mind that's constantly rewired by chaos.

You can't hear God clearly when you're spiritually multitasking.

The discipline of focus is not about withdrawal from the world, it's about choosing what gets access to your mental real estate.

It's not isolation. It's intentionality.

It's saying, "My peace is too precious to rent out to noise."

SACRED STILLNESS

Silence is not empty, it's sacred.

It's the place where God restores your perspective and resets your priorities.

When you turn down the noise, conviction gets louder.

When you slow your pace, revelation catches up.

That's why Jesus often withdrew to pray.

He wasn't escaping people, He was re-centering His attention on the Father.

He modeled that focus isn't automatic; it's cultivated.

And if even Jesus needed to unplug from the crowd to stay aligned with His purpose, so do we.

PRACTICAL WISDOM FOR A FOCUSED LIFE

Set digital boundaries. Schedule time to be offline. Let your soul detox from constant input.

Create sacred start and stop points. Begin your day with prayer before screens; end your day with gratitude instead of scrolling.

Feed on the Word before you feed on the world. The first voice you hear shapes the rest of your day.

Righteousness in the Marketplace

Practice single-tasking. Do one thing at a time as an act of worship. Excellence is born in attention, not acceleration.

The goal isn't to eliminate technology, it's to reclaim dominion over it.

You are not a product in the marketplace of attention. You are a temple of the Holy Spirit, designed to carry peace that algorithms can't replicate.

So guard your focus like it's holy, because it is.

Your mind is not a public space; it's sacred ground.

And whoever wins your attention wins your influence.

MARTHA'S DISTRACTION AND MARY'S FOCUS: CHOOSING THE BETTER PORTION

Long before the digital age, Jesus addressed the same battle we're fighting now, the war for attention.

It didn't happen on a screen. It happened in a living room.

In Luke 10, we find two sisters: Martha and Mary.

Both loved Jesus. Both served Him.

But only one recognized what mattered most.

Martha was busy.

She was doing good things, honorable things, preparing, organizing, managing details for the Son of God Himself.

But while her hands were moving, her heart was restless.

Her work had become her worship. Her doing had replaced her being.

Mary, on the other hand, sat.

She didn't ignore responsibility. She simply recognized presence.

She discerned that the One who deserved her service desired her attention first.

And Jesus' words pierced that moment with divine simplicity:

> "MARTHA, MARTHA, YOU ARE WORRIED AND UPSET ABOUT MANY THINGS, BUT FEW THINGS ARE NEEDED, OR INDEED ONLY ONE. MARY HAS CHOSEN WHAT IS BETTER, AND IT WILL NOT BE TAKEN AWAY FROM HER." (LUKE 10:41–42, NIV)

This is not a rebuke of productivity. It's a revelation about priorities.

Jesus wasn't condemning Martha's work; He was confronting her worry.

He wasn't criticizing her motion; He was calling out her misalignment.

Because in the Kingdom, proximity without presence still counts as distraction.

You can be close to Jesus and still miss Him if your attention is divided.

THE SPIRITUAL PSYCHOLOGY OF DISTRACTION

Martha's story shows us what happens when anxiety disguises itself as responsibility.

Her activity was rooted in fear, the fear of not doing enough, not being enough, not meeting expectations.

That same fear drives much of our digital busyness today.

We scroll to stay relevant. We post to stay

visible. We consume to stay informed, but end up starving spiritually.

Jesus wasn't just teaching two sisters; He was teaching us how to manage modern life.

He was saying: You can't hear Me clearly if you don't slow down long enough to listen.

Attention is the gateway to revelation.

And when your attention is constantly fractured, your discernment will always be foggy.

THE BETTER PORTION

Mary chose the better portion, not the easier one.

It takes faith to sit when the world says strive.

It takes trust to be still when culture says

produce.

It takes maturity to pause in a generation that equates silence with insignificance.

But the better portion is not found in perfection. It's found in presence.

And presence is where wisdom lives.

If you want to hear God clearly in a noisy world, you must build altars of stillness.

You must choose moments of quiet, not as luxury, but as loyalty, to the One who still whispers in the wind.

Because the wisdom you seek will not come through constant motion.

It will come through focused devotion.

And when you finally slow down long enough to sit at His feet, you'll realize that what He wanted all along was not your performance, it was your attention.

Dig Deeper

Take a moment to quiet your mind before you begin.

Breathe. Let the noise settle.

Now, read these questions slowly, not to finish them, but to feel them.

They are meant to pull you back into the sacred space where wisdom lives.

1. **Attention as Worship:**

    Where does your attention naturally go when you're anxious, lonely, or uncertain?

    What does that reveal about what you truly worship in those moments?

2. **Digital Boundaries:**

    How often do you invite God into your digital spaces, your scrolling, your posting, your learning?

    Would He recognize His voice in the tone, pace, and posture of your online presence?

3. **Noise vs. Stillness:**

   When was the last time you sat in silence with no background music, no phone, no distraction, just God?

   What emotions surfaced in that quiet? What did they expose?

4. **Martha or Mary:**

   In your daily rhythm, where do you see more of Martha, busyness, worry, striving?

   And where do you make room to be like Mary, sitting, listening, receiving?

   What would it look like to choose the better portion today?

5. **Spiritual Discernment:**

   How can you tell the difference between discernment and suspicion in your own life?

What patterns or voices influence how you interpret truth online?

6. **Focus and Formation:**

    What has been shaping your thinking lately, Scripture or social media?

    What practical boundaries can you set this week to renew your focus and reclaim your peace?

7. **Presence Over Performance:**

    What is one area of your life or business where you've been performing instead of being present?

    How might God be inviting you to slow down and simply sit with Him there?

ANCHORED IN WISDOM

Father,

In a world that never stops talking, teach us how to listen.

In a culture that rewards noise, train our hearts to value stillness.

Let wisdom, not worry, become the rhythm of our lives.

We repent for every moment we traded presence for productivity,

for every time we sought relevance more than revelation,

for every hour we gave away to distraction when You were waiting in the quiet.

We return our minds to You.

Our focus. Our feed. Our attention. Our appetite.

Every tab open in our hearts, we close them now and make space for You again.

Give us discernment that is pure, not paranoid.

Give us curiosity that is holy, not carnal.

Righteousness in the Marketplace

Give us the kind of focus that silences fear and multiplies fruit.
Help us to think with Heaven while we live in the digital world.
Let every word we speak, every system we build, every post we share
carry the fragrance of Your Spirit and the peace of Your wisdom.
May we be known not for how loud we are,
but for how anchored we remain when everything else is shaking.
We don't want artificial intelligence without divine understanding.
We don't want innovation without integrity.
We don't want information without intimacy.
We want You,
the Wisdom who became flesh,

the Word who walked among us,

the Light that no darkness can consume.

Teach us to lead minds and shape systems without losing our souls.

Teach us to feed people truth instead of trends.

Teach us to stay human, humble, and holy in a world addicted to performance.

Let wisdom be our witness.

Let discernment be our defense.

And let wholeness, real wholeness, be the mark of every righteous builder You raise in this generation.

In Jesus' name,

Amen.

Righteousness in the Marketplace

PART IV - THE FINAL AUDIT

CHAPTER 10

THE UNSEEN FRUIT OF RIGHTEOUS WORK

QUIET FRUIT: WHAT GROWS WHEN NO ONE'S WATCHING

Sometimes the greatest proof of partnership with God isn't what you build, it's what grows long after you've left. Years ago, God sent me to a small mining town in another state. On paper, it made no sense. The move was uncomfortable, the finances were tight, and the warfare was intense. But heaven had an assignment. In prayer, the Lord began to show me what He longed to do in that region. He invited me to decree restoration over a place that looked beyond repair.

So I prayed. Quietly. Hidden. No hashtags, no announcements, just whispered obedience. I declared family flourishing where there had been addiction, prosperity where there had been poverty, and revival where there had been decay. And then I waited.

Years later, long after I had returned home, I began to see the fruit surface.

The very things He told me to decree were being fulfilled in real time.

Corrupt ministries had been dismantled. Healthy ones had taken root.

The economy was reviving. Buildings once

abandoned were being restored.

Family-friendly events replaced drunken festivals.

New leaders were emerging with integrity and vision, people who loved the town and wanted to serve, not be seen.

And in that moment, I didn't feel pride. I felt awe.

God had loved that town so much that He rearranged my entire life to send me there for a season.

He inconvenienced me to bless them.

He invited me to lay my life down for strangers so they could encounter His mercy.

That realization brought a joy that words can barely hold, the joy of knowing Heaven keeps promises even when no one applauds.

The spiritual lesson from that season still anchors me:

It's not what you can see on the surface that counts, it's the foundation beneath. Now, decades later, the quiet fruit that defines my life isn't revival statistics or public influence, it's peace.

Peace that surpasses understanding.

Peace that holds steady through loss, criticism, abundance, and scarcity.

Peace that whispers, God is enough.

I used to equate fruit with outcomes, numbers, growth, recognition.

Now I see it in what remains when everything else shakes.

Peace, contentment, and faithfulness have become the real harvest.

They are the evidence of righteousness planted deep.

Because when your foundation is obedience, the fruit doesn't have to announce itself.

It simply appears, quietly, beautifully, in God's timing.

GENERATIONAL INHERITANCE

When I think of legacy, I don't think of buildings or brands.

I think of souls.

Not just the ones I'll never meet on this side of eternity,

but the ones closest to me, my children, my husband, my family, my friends, the people God allows my life to brush against for a moment in time.

Because legacy, in Heaven's language, isn't about what we leave behind.

It's about who we helped lead forward.

> *"I COULD HAVE NO GREATER JOY THAN TO HEAR THAT MY CHILDREN ARE FOLLOWING THE TRUTH."*
> *, 3 JOHN 1:4 (NLT)*

Every business, every book, every act of service, they are all just vehicles.

Temporary tools used to reach eternal hearts.

If what I build doesn't transform a soul, then it's just structure without substance.

True inheritance isn't stored in a bank account or a storage unit.

It's stored in Heaven, where moth and rust can't touch it.

> *"DON'T STORE UP TREASURES HERE ON EARTH, WHERE MOTHS EAT THEM AND RUST DESTROYS THEM...*
> *STORE YOUR TREASURES IN HEAVEN, WHERE MOTHS AND RUST CANNOT DESTROY, AND THIEVES DO NOT BREAK IN AND STEAL."*
> *, MATTHEW 6:19-20 (NLT)*

My greatest inheritance for obedience is simple:

That when I stand before the Lord, I hear Him say, "Well done, My good and faithful servant." (Matthew 25:21)

And behind me, I see a multitude, people whose lives were changed, healed, or awakened through the quiet work God called me to do.

If even one million souls were reached because I said yes in hidden places,

that will be my legacy.

There was a moment, years ago, that reminded me what legacy really looks like.

Back when I owned a skincare company, I received a message from a woman, a Muslim woman, living in a country where faith was dangerous and freedom was limited.

She told me, "Pray to your God that I can

get out of this country and bring my family with me safely."

So I prayed.

Two months later, she wrote back.

Her words still echo in my spirit:

"Your God heard my prayer. My children and I are safe in a new country. Your God is real."

I wept.

Because in that moment, I realized that legacy had nothing to do with my products or profits.

It had everything to do with partnership, with being trusted to introduce someone to a God who saves.

That woman and her family are my inheritance.

And the people they will touch, the generations that will be changed because of their deliverance, are part of that legacy too.

That's what righteousness in business looks like.

It multiplies beyond what we can count.

It ripples across borders and generations.

It reminds us that God doesn't just bless what we build,

He blesses why we build it.

> "THOSE WHO ARE WISE WILL SHINE AS BRIGHT AS THE SKY, AND THOSE WHO LEAD MANY TO RIGHTEOUSNESS WILL SHINE LIKE THE STARS FOREVER."
> , DANIEL 12:3 (NLT)

Because at the end of the day, the greatest generational wealth is not gold.

It's faith.

It's testimony.

It's the eternal echo of one soul saying, "Your God is real."

HEAVEN'S REPORT CARD

When we talk about Heaven's report card, it's not a metaphor.

Heaven is recording everything.

Every word. Every motive. Every act of obedience and every act of disobedience.

Nothing escapes God's record.

But the difference grace makes is astounding.

Because when we come to Christ, the record doesn't vanish , it's covered.

Our sins are still known, but they're no longer counted.

The blood of Jesus stands between our failures and the Father's sight, so what He sees when He looks at us is not our history, it's His Son.

This is the mystery of grace: we've been justified by the blood, but sanctification is the life we live in response to it.

Justification happens once, when we accept Jesus as Lord and Savior, we're declared righteous in God's sight (Romans 5:1).

Sanctification is the process that follows, the daily yielding, the continual refining, the lifelong participation in holiness as we let the Spirit shape our character into the likeness of Christ (1 Thessalonians 4:3).

It's not about perfection. It's about participation.

God does the cleansing, but we must do the surrendering.

And when we live this way, repentant, forgiving, humble, and obedient, the

Father's record doesn't show our performance; it shows Christ's perfection credited to our account.

Every act of obedience is marked "paid in full" by the blood of the Lamb.

That's why Heaven's definition of success is so different from ours.

Success on earth is measured in outcomes. Success in Heaven is measured in obedience.

It's the one soul saved.

The one act of repentance.

The quiet forgiveness extended to someone who didn't deserve it.

The hard yes to God when every part of you wanted to say no.

These are the grades that Heaven records with joy.

Jesus warned us about the danger of counterfeit success when He said,

Righteousness in the Marketplace

> *"MANY WILL SAY TO ME IN THAT DAY, 'LORD, LORD, HAVE WE NOT PROPHESIED IN YOUR NAME, CAST OUT DEMONS IN YOUR NAME, AND DONE MANY WONDERS IN YOUR NAME?' AND THEN I WILL DECLARE TO THEM, 'I NEVER KNEW YOU; DEPART FROM ME, YOU WHO PRACTICE LAWLESSNESS.'"*
> *, MATTHEW 7:22–23 (NKJV)*

That verse has always pierced me deeply.

Because it shows that fruit without intimacy is failure in God's eyes.

Ministry, business, miracles, none of it counts if it wasn't birthed from obedience and love.

There have been seasons where, by worldly standards, it looked like I had failed , plans collapsed, doors closed, projects went unseen.

But Heaven was smiling.

Because God doesn't grade outcomes.

He grades obedience.

And the peace that comes from knowing He's pleased, that's worth more than applause, accolades, or influence.

If we truly want Heaven's reward, we have to become what I call dead men walking, dead to self, alive in Christ.

Because only when self is silenced can Christ reign.

Only then can we work, lead, and live in a way that Heaven recognizes as righteous.

That's Heaven's report card.

It's not about how much we achieved, but about how much we yielded.

It's not about how many followed us, but how faithfully we followed Him.

LIVING FOR THE LONG HAUL

Living for the long haul isn't about endurance alone, it's about eternity. Everything we do on this earth is being deposited somewhere: into the account of Heaven or the account of hell. Every word, every motive, every choice is shaping eternal consequence.

To live for the long haul is to live with eternity in view. It's to remember that righteousness is not a sprint toward success but a slow, sacred obedience that leaves generations better than we found them. Whether that legacy is spiritual, financial, or intellectual, it begins with how we show up in the present, how much we're willing to renew our minds and die to self so that Christ can reign in us.

I've learned this through experience, not theory.

When I was sixteen, God spared my life after an overdose that could have ended everything. That moment anchored me in gratitude so deep that every breath since then has felt like a gift. That's what keeps me steady when fruit takes years to appear. I've already received the greatest miracle, life itself, and everything since has been grace upon grace.

But I've also learned that God often asks us to take the long route.

When I owned my skincare company, the business was thriving. We had associates in multiple states, international sales, and a growing customer base. But in the middle of that success, my health began to fail. I heard the Lord say, "Do you trust Me?"

When I said yes, He said, "Then close the business. It's either your health or this store, and if you choose this business, it will kill you."

That was one of the hardest yeses of my life.

It felt like burying my own child. Yet that act of obedience saved my life and preserved the future God had waiting for me. I had to surrender what was thriving in order to survive. I had to take the long road so I could still be here to walk it. Looking back now, I understand that the long road is never punishment, it's preparation.

Sometimes God slows us down not because of disobedience, but because He's developing the strength, stamina, and spiritual maturity to sustain what He's building through us. Just as He told Israel,

"I will not drive them out before you in a single year... little by little I will drive them out before you, until you have increased enough to take possession of the land" (Exodus 23:29-30).

EVEN PROMISE REQUIRES PROCESS.

David lived that truth.

He was anointed king long before he wore the crown. For years he served Saul, hid in caves, and endured betrayal, all while carrying a promise he couldn't yet touch. That wasn't delay. It was development. The wilderness was God's classroom for kingship.

It's the same with us.

If the promise came too soon, it would crush us.

If the blessing arrived before the

backbone, it would break us.

So God gives it little by little, until we grow into the person who can carry it with humility and endurance.

The long haul is not glamorous. It's refining.

But it's where we learn that maturity isn't measured by speed, it's measured by surrender.

If I could give one sentence of counsel to the weary, it would be this:

LEARN TO GROW INTO THE PERSON WHO CAN SUSTAIN THE BLESSING.

That takes time, and time is mercy. Because time allows transformation to take root so that when the promise comes, it won't destroy you, it will reveal you.

Dig Deeper

Take this section slowly. These questions are not for quick answers but for honest communion with God. Let the Holy Spirit search the hidden places while you write.

Quiet Fruit

Where in my life has obedience produced unseen fruit?

Have I dismissed any season as failure that Heaven might actually call fruitful?

Generational Inheritance

How is my work shaping souls, in my home, my business, and my community?

What am I intentionally passing down that cannot be spent or stolen?

Heaven's Report Card

When God reviews my motives, what will He see: ambition or obedience?

Where is the Holy Spirit inviting me to exchange performance for intimacy?

Living for the Long Haul

Am I willing to take the slow route if it means growing into the promise rather than rushing ahead of it?

How do I respond when God asks me to release something that's thriving in order to preserve something eternal?

Legacy that Lasts

What fruit of my life will still speak after I'm gone?

What will Heaven remember because I said yes when it would have been easier to quit?

Let your answers become prayers. Let your prayers become action. And let your actions become the quiet fruit that testifies of righteousness long after your name is forgotten , but His remains.

ETERNAL HARVEST

Father,
 teach us to build with eternity in mind.
 When our hearts crave applause, remind us that Heaven's silence is often Your approval.
 When the harvest seems hidden, remind us that unseen fruit still feeds nations.
 Help us measure success by obedience, not by outcome, by faithfulness, not fame.

We surrender every seed we've sown in tears, trusting that You will water it in ways we may never see.

We release every field that feels barren, believing You're cultivating what time cannot destroy.

And we choose to labor not for the crowns of men, but for the commendation that only You can give:

"Well done, My good and faithful servant." Let our businesses become vineyards of righteousness.

Let our words carry weight in eternity.

Let our hidden obedience echo louder than our public success.

Father, when history forgets our names, let Heaven remember our fruit.

And let every legacy we leave whisper the same truth,

that righteousness was worth it all.

Amen.

Righteousness in the Marketplace

CHAPTER 11

WHAT WILL HEAVEN SAY ABOUT WHAT YOU BUILT?

BUILDING WITH ETERNITY IN MIND

I've grown up in church most of my life. Even though there was a period as a teenager when I walked away from the Lord, everything changed when I was sixteen. I overdosed, and God came and rescued me from what felt like the pit of hell. That encounter was real. It was tangible. It was life changing. And it put the fear of the Lord in me in a way I will never forget.

But if I'm being honest, the most memorable moment where the fear of the Lord became present in my life, specifically in my business life, happened during my skin care business days. There was a woman from a Muslim country who followed me on social media. She told me she was fleeing her country, leaving first to establish safety, and then her family would follow after. She did not ask me to pray in a vague way. She was very direct. She said, "I need you to pray to your God that my family comes with me safely."

So I prayed to Jesus, the one and only true God. Two months went by and I did not hear anything, but I kept praying. Then she messaged me again and said, "Your God heard your prayers and answered. My family is now with me and we are all safe." And she gave glory to Jesus.

That moment shook me in the best way. Because she lived in a country where even if I wanted to sell my skin care products, I could not. Sanctions and trade agreements would not allow it. She was not following me because she wanted to buy soap. She was not following me because of my personality, or my looks, or how impressive I seemed. She reached out to me because of my God.

And in that moment I realized just how powerful a business platform really is.

My business was not just a way to make money. It was a public witness. Every interaction was speaking. Everything I said, everything I did, how I carried myself, what I spoke about, how I spoke about it, how I treated customers, how I handled conflict, how I responded under pressure, all of it was preaching a message I was not sitting down to "study" first. That is why Paul's words hit so hard, because he makes it plain that our lives are being read.

> "CLEARLY, YOU YOURSELVES ARE OUR LETTER OF RECOMMENDATION, WRITTEN IN OUR HEARTS, TO BE KNOWN AND READ BY ALL. YOU SHOW THAT YOU ARE A LETTER FROM CHRIST, THE RESULT OF OUR MINISTRY AMONG YOU. THIS LETTER IS WRITTEN NOT WITH PEN AND INK, BUT WITH THE SPIRIT OF THE LIVING GOD. IT IS CARVED NOT ON TABLETS OF

> *STONE, BUT ON HUMAN HEARTS." (2 CORINTHIANS 3:2–3, NLT)*

So the question becomes simple, and it is not comfortable.

IF MY LIFE IS BEING READ, THEN WHAT ARE PEOPLE READING?

That experience taught me that I needed to strive to walk with integrity, not just in obvious "church" areas, but in the small details of everyday business life. It made me want to deal with the issues in my own heart, my own patterns, my own reactions, and my own blind spots, because sometimes it is not just sin that destroys people. Sin is one thing, and we all have to deal with sin. But sometimes it is the unresolved issues of life, the wounds, the pride, the offense, the need to be right, the need to be seen, the need to win, that will quietly push us into compromise if we are not careful. And those compromises do not just affect us. They can lead someone else into sin too.

That is when the fear of the Lord became real for me in business.

Not as terror, and not as religious performance, but as a holy awareness that God is involved, that He is watching, and that He cares about how I represent Him. Because whether I like it or not, my life is a letter. My business is a letter. My leadership is a letter.

And people are reading it.

STEWARDSHIP OVER SPECTACLE

One of the biggest mistakes I made, and one I see many believers make, is assuming that building well automatically means learning how to market better.

We want to honor God, so we look for wisdom. We study strategy. We learn platforms. We learn systems. We learn how to grow. And none of that is wrong in itself.

The problem comes when the voices we learn from are operating from a hustle mindset, even when they say they are not. Some of them are believers. Some of them are not. But the fruit is the same.

Mammon is still driving the machine.

And without realizing it, we begin allowing human expertise to override God's instruction.

I did that.

I took advice that worked. I want to be honest about that. It produced numbers. It produced engagement. It produced income. But it also produced something else in me. Pride. Exhaustion. Anxiety. A constant sense that I was behind and had to catch up.

That is how spectacle sneaks in.

Spectacle looks like success, but it demands everything from you. Your time. Your peace. Your presence. Eventually, even your joy.

Stewardship is quieter. Stewardship asks different questions. Not just, "Does this work?" but, "What is this doing to my soul?"

There was a season where I realized my business was starting to affect my family. I was irritated when interrupted. I was strict with my time in a way that left no margin for people I loved. And that was my warning sign, because the people under my roof matter more than any metric ever will.

That is when conviction set in.

And here is what I learned the hard way.

God does not compete with hustle. He withdraws from it.

Scripture tells us plainly that God resists pride, even when it wears spiritual clothing.

> "GOD OPPOSES THE PROUD BUT GIVES GRACE TO THE HUMBLE."
> JAMES 4:6 (NLT)

Humility is not thinking less of yourself.

Humility is knowing who you depend on.

That is why Scripture also warns us not to inflate our sense of importance.

> "DON'T THINK YOU ARE BETTER THAN YOU REALLY ARE. BE HONEST IN YOUR EVALUATION OF YOURSELVES, MEASURING YOURSELVES BY THE FAITH GOD HAS GIVEN US."
> ROMANS 12:3 (NLT)

Spectacle trains you to think higher of yourself than you ought to. Stewardship trains you to remember where everything came from.

This is where Sabbath began to confront me, not as a rule, but as a revelation.

The Sabbath is not about a calendar day. It is about posture.

When God commanded rest, He was teaching trust.

"REMEMBER THE SABBATH DAY BY KEEPING IT HOLY… FOR IN SIX DAYS THE LORD MADE THE HEAVENS AND THE EARTH, BUT ON THE SEVENTH DAY HE RESTED. THAT IS WHY THE LORD BLESSED THE SABBATH DAY AND SET IT APART AS HOLY."
EXODUS 20:8, 11 (NLT)

And again, God explains the heart behind it:

> *"REMEMBER THAT YOU WERE ONCE SLAVES IN EGYPT, BUT THE LORD YOUR GOD BROUGHT YOU OUT... THAT IS WHY THE LORD YOUR GOD HAS COMMANDED YOU TO REST."*
> *DEUTERONOMY 5:15 (NLT)*

Rest was meant to break slavery thinking.

Hustle says, "If I stop, everything falls apart."

Sabbath says, "God is holding this, not me."

That is why Scripture also reminds us where provision truly comes from.

> *"REMEMBER THE LORD YOUR GOD. HE IS THE ONE WHO GIVES YOU POWER TO BE SUCCESSFUL."*
> *DEUTERONOMY 8:18 (NLT)*

If God gives the power to make wealth, then there are ways of living that can shut that power off. Self reliance. Arrogance. Forgetting Him.

This is exactly what happened to the church of Laodicea.

Jesus said:

> *"YOU SAY, 'I AM RICH. I HAVE EVERYTHING I WANT. I DON'T NEED A THING!' AND YOU DON'T REALIZE THAT YOU ARE WRETCHED AND MISERABLE AND POOR AND BLIND AND NAKED."*
> REVELATION 3:17 (NLT)

Laodicea was not lukewarm because they stopped going to church. They were lukewarm because they stopped depending on God.

Historically, Laodicea was one of the wealthiest cities of its time. When a massive earthquake destroyed the city around AD 60, Rome offered financial aid to rebuild. Laodicea refused. They rebuilt the entire city with their own money. They did not need help.

And that was the problem.

They were technologically advanced. Financially strong. Medically innovative. And spiritually self sufficient.

Jesus did not rebuke them for being wealthy. He rebuked them for forgetting Him.

Spectacle produces independence from God.

Stewardship produces intimacy with God.

That is the difference.

God was protecting me when He pulled me out of hustle. He was protecting my marriage. My children. My heart. My calling.

Because hustle does not just exhaust you. It hardens you.

It turns relationships into interruptions. People into obstacles. Conversations into transactions.

Stewardship keeps people human.

Stewardship says, "My business exists to serve people, not consume them."

Stewardship says, "My success cannot cost my family."

Stewardship says, "If God did not ask for it, I do not need it."

That is why I build differently now.

Not because this way is superior, but because it is obedient.

Spectacle wants applause.

Stewardship wants heaven's approval.

And those two paths rarely look the same.

THE WEIGHT OF RESPONSIBILITY

For me, the weight of responsibility is not something I became aware of later in life. It has been with me since I was very young.

Righteousness in the Marketplace

I grew up in church, and whether people agree with the way that teaching was delivered or not, one thing was drilled into us early on: your life speaks. Your actions preach. Someone is always watching. Long before I had my personal encounter with the Lord, long before I was truly serving Him, I understood that influence carries weight.

Even as a teenager, when I was not walking with God, I could see it plainly. My peers watched me closely. They mimicked my behavior. They picked up my language, my attitudes, my choices. They came to me for advice, for affirmation, for direction. That alone was sobering. I realized that leadership does not require a title. Influence does not wait for maturity. Whether I wanted it or not, what I did mattered to someone else.

That awareness never left me.

As I grew older, it only deepened. Because influence does not stop with peers. It starts at home. It starts with the people who live under your roof. My children are watching me. My husband is watching me. My neighbors are watching me. Friends, extended family, coworkers, even strangers online who never comment or engage. They are watching.

Every interaction communicates something.

How I speak to people.

How I treat those who disagree with me.

How I respond when I am tired, frustrated, or interrupted.

How I talk about God.

How I talk about others.

How I carry myself in public and in private.

How I show up online.

How I conduct business.

How I correct.

How I repent.

All of it speaks.

And whether I see the outcome or not, whether anyone ever tells me or not, my life is either drawing someone closer to Christ or pushing them further away. There is no neutral ground. Silence speaks. Tone speaks. Absence speaks. So does presence.

This is why accountability before God is not theoretical for me. It is personal. I do not have the luxury of pretending my choices only affect me. They never have. Leadership is not just about authority. It is about responsibility. Responsibility for how your words land. Responsibility for the atmosphere you create. Responsibility for whether people encounter the character of Christ through you or encounter something distorted and wounded instead.

That realization has shaped how I live, how I lead, and how I build. Not perfectly. I still miss the mark. I still have to repent. I still have to realign. But I do not get to forget that my life is speaking even when my mouth is closed.

And one day, I will give an account for what it said.

FAITHFUL WHEN THE SPOTLIGHT FADES

When the spotlight fades, what disappears first is not the work. It is the attention. The numbers. The praise. The momentum. The sense that someone is watching and validating every step you take.

That is usually when people quit. Or compromise. Or numb out.

For me, what keeps me faithful when none of that is there is not discipline or fear or willpower. It is encounter.

The encounter I had with God at sixteen years old did not expire. It did not fade with time. It did not lose its weight as life got busier or more complex. I still walk with the same God who met me in that hospital room, the same God who pulled me out of the pit when I could not save myself. That reality is what anchors me when building feels heavy, when business feels thankless, and when obedience costs more than it gives.

Because there are days when this work feels like too much. Anyone who has built something from the ground up knows that. There are seasons where it feels like swimming upstream with no shoreline in sight. You work, you serve, you give, you build, and still wonder if it is worth it. That is when temptation creeps in, not always as obvious sin, but as resentment, isolation, compromise, or emotional shutdown.

And when no one is watching, it would be easy to justify any of it.

What I have learned is this. I do not survive those moments by becoming more self sufficient. I survive them by becoming more honest. I go to God first. Not to perform. Not to polish. I bare my soul. I tell Him the truth about my thoughts, my exhaustion, my frustration, and my weakness. Prayer for me is not optional. It is survival.

But prayer is not just talking. It is listening. It is sitting long enough to hear what God actually wants to say back. It is refusing to rush Him for answers. Repentance is part of that rhythm. Not as shame, but as alignment. Accountability is part of it too, but not outsourced. I hold myself accountable first because I know God sees everything anyway.

At the end of the day, I am not performing for an audience of thousands. I am performing for an audience of One.

That reality sobers you. Because one day I will stand before Him and look Him in the eyes, and there will be no branding, no metrics, no excuses. Just truth. Just obedience or the lack of it.

My life has been shaped by obedience that no one applauded. Not just in small acts of generosity, but in the places I lived, the jobs I took or refused, the doors I closed, and the income I walked away from. I have said no to opportunities that would have elevated my visibility and my bank account. Some of those opportunities came from people whose names you would recognize today.

But I could not trade my soul for access. I have seen hell. I know how real it is. And while fear of hell is not what drives my obedience, love does. The love of a God who went to unfathomable lengths to save me. How could I treat that gift casually. How could I throw it away for comfort, money, influence, or applause.

I am not against success. I am not against wealth. I am not against visibility or influence. None of those things are the issue. The issue is cost. The issue is what it does to your soul and the souls of others along the way.

I will not exchange salvation for status. I will not sell obedience for approval. I will not trade gratitude for convenience. Faithfulness when the spotlight fades is not about being strong. It is about remembering what you were rescued from and Who rescued you. And choosing, again and again, to honor that gift no matter who is watching.

WHAT WILL HEAVEN REMEMBER ME BY?

When I strip everything down to its core, I know this with certainty: what I built, led, or accomplished was never the point. The purpose was worship. The purpose was obedience. The purpose was that through my life, in visible and invisible ways, souls would come to know Him.

Righteousness in the Marketplace

At the end of my life, there is only one sentence I want to hear.

"Well done, my good and faithful servant."

Not well known.

Not well followed.

Not well funded.

Faithful.

I do not want to leave behind a legacy where people curse God because of me. I need to be very clear about that. If someone rejects God because they are offended by righteousness, that is between them and the Lord. I cannot control that. But if someone walks away from God because I mistreated them, misled them, exploited them, bullied them, rejected them, or used them for my own gain, that is a different matter entirely. That is a weight I refuse to carry.

That kind of legacy would grieve heaven.

Righteousness in the Marketplace

My vision has never changed. It has simply been refined. One million souls in heaven. Not because of my name, my brand, or my visibility, but because somewhere along the way, through my words, my obedience, my leadership, my correction, my love, or the seeds I planted in others, they encountered God.

And when I say seeds, I do not mean money alone. I mean truth spoken when it was uncomfortable. Encouragement given when it cost me something. Leadership that chose responsibility over applause. Love that did not manipulate. Correction that did not dominate. Presence that did not perform.

Right now, I do not feel torn between obedience and ambition. That tension used to exist, but it does not rule me anymore. I have learned to recognize that my life is not my own. I am, in the truest sense, a dead woman walking.

I die to myself daily. Not out of pride. Not out of performance. Not out of some spiritual badge of honor. But because I genuinely understand that I belong to Him. That understanding is one of the reasons this book was hard to write. It is one of the reasons building this business has required such deep surrender. All I want, if I am being honest, is to remain in His presence. But I also recognize that obedience requires movement. It requires communication. It requires follow through. Wanting to be with Him is not disobedience, but refusing to do what He asked because it costs comfort would be. So if heaven remembers anything about my work, I hope it remembers this:

That I did it as unto the Lord.

Not unto people.

Not unto platforms.

Not unto outcomes.

Unto Him.

And if that is all heaven records about me, it will be more than enough.

The End

A FINAL INVITATION

If this book resonated with you and you want to continue exploring what it looks like to live and work with integrity, obedience, and depth, I invite you to visit FeJonesLive.com.

While this book focused on righteousness in the marketplace, my work extends beyond business alone. I equip high achieving women to fulfill their God given assignment through the integration of faith, psychology, functional health, and human resilience. This work is rooted in the belief that wholeness matters, and that clarity of mind, stewardship of the body, and spiritual maturity are not separate pursuits but deeply connected.

One on one coaching opportunities are limited, but I have created a growing collection of resources designed to support women who want to learn, reflect, and grow at their own pace. These include books, workbooks, a podcast, weekly articles on my blog, and a private membership library called The Study Room hosted on Patreon.

The Study Room is a self paced private learning library for readers and listeners who want deeper, more structured study beyond my free blog and podcast. Each learning series is built around a specific theme and includes research based insights and practical tools drawn from functional health, psychology, faith, and human resilience.

This is not a coaching program or a live community. All content is self directed and designed for quiet learning, thoughtful application, and long term growth.

Wherever this book finds you, my hope is that it encourages you to build with eternity in mind and to walk out your calling with clarity, humility, and courage.

Thank you for reading.

www.ingramcontent.com/pod-product-compliance
Lightning Source LLC
Chambersburg PA
CBHW021759220426
43662CB00006B/120